ORCHID MODERN

ORCHID MODERN

LIVING & DESIGNING
with the WORLD'S MOST
ELEGANT HOUSEPLANTS

MARC HACHADOURIAN
CURATOR OF THE ORCHID COLLECTION

NEW YORK BOTANICAL GARDEN

PHOTOGRAPHS BY CLAIRE ROSEN

Published in 2019 by Timber Press, Inc.,
in association with The New York Botanical Garden
The Haseltine Building
133 S.W. Second Avenue, Suite 450
Portland, Oregon 97204-3527
timberpress.com

Printed in China
Text and cover design by Adrianna Sutton

ISBN 978-1-60469-816-9
Catalog records for this book are available
from the Library of Congress and the British Library.

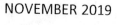

To my partner, family, friends, and teachers—thank you
for inspiring me on my journey and always believing
in that little boy who loved flowers.

Discovering the World of Orchids • 9

Keeping Orchids Happy and Healthy • 31

Seasonal Care Calendar • 81

Orchid Projects • 91

Easy-Care Orchids from A to Z • 151

Resources • 237

Photo and Illustration Credits • 241

Index • 242

JEWEL ORCHID TERRARIUM

93

DECORATIVE ORCHID TERRARIUM

97

ORCHID PENJING

121

WOODLAND GARDEN ORCHID CENTERPIECE

127

CONTENTS

ORCHID WREATH **103**

ORCHID KOKEDAMA **109**

ORCHID BONSAI TREE **115**

MINIATURE ORCHID MOBILE **133**

ORCHID SCULPTURE **139**

HANGING ORCHID GALLERY **145**

Discovering the *World of* ORCHIDS

MAYBE YOUR FIRST ORCHID was a gift from a friend or an impulse purchase
at the checkout counter, where you succumbed to the allure of the blooms and took
the plunge to bring your first plant home. It all starts with just one orchid. Although
H. G. Wells's short story "The Flowering of the Strange Orchid" is a fantasy about a
carnivorous plant, it is also a metaphor for the obsessive collecting that orchids have
inspired throughout history. If you are a lover of plants and flowers, orchids have a
way of working themselves into your life.

The universal exotic appeal of orchids is strong, tempting gardeners into test-
ing their skills with orchid growing. This pastime is often portrayed as the ultimate
achievement in horticultural skill that should only be attempted by the most expert
gardeners. Over time, however, their complex biology has been slowly unraveled,
their propagation mastered, and we now understand that orchids are far from the
fussy, difficult, or impossible plants that their reputation makes them out to be.
Orchids are no longer rarities that have to be sought out from specialty nurseries;
they have become almost ubiquitous floral decorations. They are different from other
plants, but with a foundation of knowledge about their history, ecology, and diversity, any home gardener or houseplant enthusiast can succeed with the right orchid.

After a few attempts, the story may turn to an admission of failure and a resignation that you'll never succeed with orchids. But a failure to succeed with a plant should be viewed as an opportunity to learn and not a cause for shame. You needn't stealthily hide the limp lifeless body of your latest orchid victim out of sight under last week's trash. Like learning to cook, growing orchids allows you to refine your skills, learn from your mistakes, and enjoy the fruits of your labors. Whether you have a single orchid or an ever-expanding army of plants, orchid growing can be a rewarding experience that brings years of enjoyment.

THE HISTORY OF ORCHID CULTIVATION

Although they have experienced a recent surge in popularity, orchids have been revered and prized horticultural subjects for thousands of years. The widespread natural distribution of orchid species has intersected with human history all across the globe, with each society discovering and creating their own mythos and incorporating their native orchid flora into their culture and horticulture. As global exploration became more commonplace, the beautiful and exotic orchid flora of the world became the horticultural status symbols and icons they are today.

In Chinese texts dating back to 500 B.C., orchids had cultural significance, with the plants being prized for their beauty and fragrance. Several species of native orchids were used in Chinese herbal medicine, but it was mainly *Dendrobium* and *Cymbidium* orchids that captured the interests of gardeners. The Chinese believed that the plants' powerful sweet fragrance could be used to ward off evil forest spirits if the blooms were plucked and worn in the hair. Orchids started to grow in popularity as nobility took an interest in them, and they were often depicted in traditional Chinese decorative arts. The graceful foliage and blooms were elegantly portrayed and used as a popular motif in paintings, ceramics, and carvings. Even the Chinese word for orchid, *lan*, was associated with things or people that were exceptional. The famous Chinese philosopher Confucius referred to orchids as superior flowers and associated them with noble acquaintances. Chinese horticulturists published texts on how to cultivate the native *Cymbidium* species that are still grown and prized by collectors today.

The Japanese have long celebrated and treasured their native flora. From wild gingers (*Asarum*) to *Hepatica* and *Rhapis* palms, the Japanese have prized their native plants and elevated their cultivation and display to an art form through the practice of *koten engei*, the cultivation of classic plants. The Japanese also have a tradition of searching out unique foliage forms, including variegated and often twisted or mutated foliage. Many of Japan's native orchid species are cultivated with a range of flower patterns, foliage forms, and variegated forms grown exclusively for their

Collected and grown for the beauty of the foliage and sweetly fragrant flowers, *Vanda falcata* has been prized by gardeners for over 400 years in its native Japan.

foliage—not their flowers. One of the most prized species, *Vanda falcata* (formerly *Neofinetia falcata*), was historically cultivated exclusively by Japanese nobility.

Many cultures in Central and South America also developed an appreciation for their native orchid flora. In many regions, blooming native orchid species were used as adornments in churches and homes during religious and other seasonal festivals. *Laelia superbiens* (Mexico), *Guarianthe skinneri* (Costa Rica), and *Miltoniopsis vexillaria* (Colombia) are still collected and cultivated for this purpose today. Species such as *Stanhopea tigrina* and *Euchile citrina* were used in traditional healing and for other ethnobotanical uses. Even modern Latin American cultures recognize the beauty and significance of orchids to their cultural identity and history, and several orchids have been adopted as national flowers: *Peristeria elata* in Panama, *Guarianthe skinneri* in Costa Rica, and *Cattleya trianae* in Colombia. The single most famous and significant orchid relationship to emerge from this part of the world was the Aztecs' discovery and use of vanilla as a flavoring, which developed into an internationally prized commodity.

In Europe and the Mediterranean region, orchids were used historically as food and medicine and were recognized as important parts of the local flora. Ancient Greeks including Theophrastus, a physician and contemporary of Aristotle who is often credited as the father of botany, noted the medicinal virtues of native terrestrial orchids. The plants were associated with having the power to increase virility and were used as an aphrodisiac, and the roots were harvested to help determine the gender of an unborn child. The paired underground tubers were considered useful in treating conditions relating to a particular part of the male anatomy, a use that gave orchids their name. The name derives from the Greek *orkhis* meaning "testicle." The procreative reference to the plants was furthered by their assumed mythical origins. Since they seemed to spontaneously appear in fields and forests, terrestrial orchids with their fantastic and often bizarre-looking flowers were believed to result from amorous encounters between Satyrs and other beasts.

It was not really until the Victorian period in Europe, however, that the modern cultivation and collecting of orchids really took root and became the horticultural phenomenon as we know it today. As global shipping routes and trade brought many natural history specimens to Europe, interest in the exotic flora and fauna sparked a revolution in natural history and biology unequaled in history. The popular fascination with exotic plants and animals was fueled by the modern mythology surrounding their discovery. The British, in particular, developed an almost insatiable desire to cultivate and possess exotic plants including ferns, palms, aroids, and of course exotic orchids brought back from all corners of the globe.

Victorian England was the perfect confluence of technology, engineering, science, and exploration to begin a wave of interest in tropical orchids from around the world. Plant collecting and cultivation became a popular and competitive pastime for both the wealthy and those wishing to emulate people of status, who built greenhouses to contain their expanding collections of plants. Massive shipments of new, exotic, and rare specimens were sent from around the world back to England and the nurseries that supplied the public's demand for orchids. Empires under glass were built to house collections of orchids and other tropical plants, with some

Many new orchid discoveries were illustrated in lavish publications, helping to fuel the demand for orchids.

of the greenhouses reaching epic proportions to house full-grown palm trees and thousands of precious plants under one glass roof. Rabid collectors such as the Duke of Devonshire, who became infected with orchid fever after falling in love with a butterfly orchid (*Psychopsis*) that bloomed in his greenhouse, sent collectors to the far reaches of the globe to bring back the newest and rarest specimens. Some orchid hunters never returned with their prized plants, becoming victims of the numerous perils awaiting them in tropical jungles. Others succeeded in their quest for new species for their own glory and that of the person who funded their expedition. Some auctioned their rarest specimens to the highest bidder, with the best and rarest plants commanding princely sums equating to tens of thousands of dollars in today's currency.

Natural history publications were popular reading at the time and included firsthand accounts of exotic travels and discovery. Naturalists such as Charles Darwin were well-known figures who were helping to unravel the mysteries of the natural world. Darwin's style of observational botany introduced readers to the marvel of plants and their biology. By studying plant movement and pollination and documenting important discoveries surrounding carnivorous plants, Darwin contributed to our understanding of so many botanical phenomena. Beyond his controversial writings on the origins of species and mankind, Darwin was also an important and early student of the orchid family, and he published the first text on

The curious blooms of *Psychopsis* orchids are credited with inspiring a mania among horticulturists and launching the Victorian obsession of collecting and growing orchids.

their pollination and biology. He was fascinated by the diversity of the orchids that grew near his home in England and the tropical orchids he cultivated in his personal greenhouse, caught under the spell of their marvelous floral forms and architecture. After observing the wondrous adaptations, tricks, and contraptions they possessed to interact with their pollinators, even Darwin, with his deep appreciation and understanding of the natural world, seemed to bestow an almost otherworldly intelligence on the plants. His seminal publication on orchid pollination, *Fertilisation of Orchids* (1862), set the foundation for scientific study on orchids and other broader concepts in biology. This publication helped build on the fashion and interest in growing orchids by teaching the public about the scientific intricacies of these exotic plants.

The Victorians set the stage for the current public fascination with orchids and solidified their reputation as fussy plants that need to be nurtured by dedicated hands in elaborate and expensive greenhouses. Orchid growing became seen as a pastime only achievable by those with cavalier spending habits and limitless resources. A lack of understanding of their basic propagation needs made orchid growing a slow and expensive hobby. Hybrids took decades to grow from seed, such that only small quantities could be produced by nurserymen, and this limited supply helped to keep the demand and prices for orchids high. Over time, however, advanced techniques for laboratory germination of orchid seeds and tissue culture allowed for the development of an orchid industry that could rapidly serve the continuous demand of hobbyists, collectors, and the cut flower industry.

Orchids are now the most popular horticultural crop in the world, surpassing even the poinsettia in popularity and sheer numbers. Tens of millions of orchid plants are produced in the United States alone, and the global market is measured in the hundreds of millions of dollars per year—not too bad of a climb for a wild forest flower that eventually grew to take over the world.

The Mass Production *of* ORCHIDS

In the early years of commercial orchid production, it could take decades of dedicated care to increase the stock of a particular plant. Breeding hybrids and growing those seeds to maturity was a slow and arduous process, and it often resulted in few if any plants reaching blooming size. Seeds were sown on muslin fiber or at the base of parent plants, and growers hoped for the best.

In 1922, the researcher Lewis Knudson developed a method to bypass the need for a specialized fungus to germinate orchid seeds. In place of the fungus, he used sterile laboratory conditions and a gelatin-like agar medium to supply the orchid seed with nutrients, allowing the embryo to germinate and grow. With this new method, thousands of seedlings could be produced from a single orchid seedpod. Knudson's germination techniques made orchid breeding on a large and commercial scale possible.

Orchid plants can be reluctant to produce offshoots. Sympodial orchids can be divided and increased more rapidly than monopodial orchids such as *Vanda* and *Phalaenopsis*, which usually only bear a single stem but may occasionally produce side branches or small plantlets for propagation. In the 1940s, researchers noted the ability of plants to be cultured using the actively growing shoot tips. These meristems could be isolated in the laboratory and grown rapidly to produce plants identical to the parent. In 1960, the French researcher Georges Morel used this technique to clone a *Cymbidium*, ushering in a new opportunity for rapid propagation of special orchids for the commercial market.

Today a single plant can be multiplied by the thousands in a short period. Technology and horticulture have enabled the orchid industry to expand and thrive. The annual profits of the orchid industry in the United States alone are nearly $300 million, with more than 36 million plants produced each year. Worldwide the value of the orchid industry has been estimated at over $1 billion. Scientific research has allowed the elite hothouse flowers of the past to become the houseplants of the future.

ORCHIDS
as Medicine *&* Food

Chinese herbal medicine uses several species of orchids. *Gastrodia elata* (tian ma), an odd orchid that does not make leaves but grows from a potato-like root, is used to treat dizziness and headaches, improve liver function, and promote blood circulation. A tea made from the dried pseudobulbs of several species including *Dendrobium nobile* (shi hu) has been used for over 2000 years to help boost gastrointestinal and kidney health. The jewel orchid *Anoectochilus* (jin xianlan) is used to help clear the lungs and to detoxify the body. Many of these medicinal orchids have been overharvested. Thankfully, however, people are starting to propagate and farm them commercially to help ease the pressures on wild plant populations and still make them available for traditional healing.

From the Aztecs of Mexico, vanilla was introduced to Europe along with chocolate in the early 1500s. The vanilla bean is not a legume at all but actually the dried and cured seedpod of the *Vanilla* orchid. Today, vanilla is the world's most popular flavor and scent and is the only orchid farmed on a large scale for something other than ornamental value. Several different species are farmed around the world, but the most commonly cultivated is *Vanilla planifolia*. Each flower has to be hand pollinated for the seedpods to develop, making vanilla farming a very labor-intensive venture and thus making vanilla one of the most expensive spices in the world, surpassed only by saffron. Either the interior of the vanilla pod is scraped or the aromatic flavor is extracted. All of those dark flecks you see in your vanilla ice cream are actually orchid seeds.

In Turkey, the traditional hot beverage salep and the frozen treat dondurma, also known as orchid ice cream, are made from the sweetened, infused, and ground tubers of terrestrial orchids. As in ancient cultures around the world, these orchid confections are believed to have a stimulating effect on the libido.

Although the source of vanilla flavoring is referred to as a vanilla bean, it's actually the seed pod of the orchid *Vanilla planifolia*.

ORCHID PLANT AND FLOWER DIVERSITY

The size and diversity of the orchid family, Orchidaceae, is nothing short of astounding, with estimates of 20,000 to 30,000 naturally occurring species. Orchids have evolved to be one of the most widespread plant families and occur naturally on every continent except Antarctica. Although we often associate orchids with tropical environments, where they have their greatest diversity, many orchids are native to the forests and fields of temperate regions and some species even range into the arctic tundra. Orchids have adapted to a wide array of habitats, including rainforests, prairies, swamps, and deserts, and a few bizarre species live their entire lives underground, only barely emerging to flower.

Orchids are regarded as being among the most highly evolved and specialized of flowering plants for the complex and sometimes bizarre relationships they have developed with their pollinators as well as their anatomical adaptations for survival. The evolutionary

Most parts of the miniature orchid *Dresslerella pilosissima*, which is native to the humid evergreen forests of Costa Rica, are covered with hairs.

diversity of orchids has created a family of plants full of extremes, ranging from some of the smallest individual flowers in the world to massive vegetable monsters. Until recently, the smallest documented orchid flowers belonged to *Platystele jungermannioides*, a minute species from Brazil with leaves only 5 mm tall and blooms only 2.5 mm in diameter. In Ecuador, scientists recently discovered an even smaller flower on a plant in the same genus; they are only 2 mm in diameter. It was discovered almost by accident by an orchid researcher who found it among the roots of another orchid he was cultivating. At the other extreme, *Vanilla* orchids can produce vines reaching more than 50 feet long that snake up tree trunks into the forest canopy. The current undisputed title of largest orchid in the world belongs to *Grammatophyllum speciosum*, a native of Indonesia that can have individual stems up to 20 feet long, with the massive plants reaching several hundred pounds over time.

Orchid seeds are the smallest plant seeds known; they can be dust-like and are often less than 1 mm long. It seems almost miraculous that anything could grow from something so small, but orchid seeds are able to germinate and grow with the aid of specialized fungi. The tiny seeds do not have any stored food, like other plant seeds, to provide the embryo with nutrients. This is where the fungus

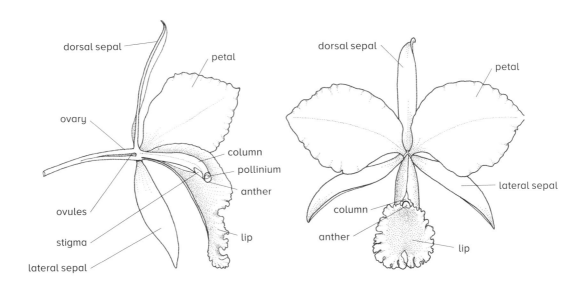

helps out. If an orchid seed lands in a location where that species' fungal partner is, the orchid seed draws nutrients from the fungus and can then germinate and grow to maturity. A delicate and surprising relationship, for sure, but how exactly does that orchid seed floating on the wind find the right fungus? The strategy that orchids have developed is to produce massive quantities of seeds, taking a shotgun approach to finding the right fungus. Each orchid seedpod can contain up to 4 million wind-dispersed seeds, thus increasing the likelihood that some will land in the right conditions for both the orchid and the fungus. This long-distance relationship is one of the reasons why orchids were historically difficult to propagate from seeds. Even now, this is something that is left for more advanced orchid growers to attempt.

Despite their huge range in plant size and shape, one trait that unites the members of Orchidaceae is their floral structure. Like most plants, orchids have flowers composed of sepals and petals, with most having three sepals and three petals. One of the petals is often modified and specialized in its color, pattern, and shape and is referred to as the lip or labellum. This petal is frequently enlarged, highly patterned, and adorned with contrasting coloration to the rest of the flower. These patterns and colors have evolved to lure in pollinators and direct them like

The inflorescence of *Rhynchostylis gigantea* bears numerous blooms that emit a spicy fragrance.

lights on a runway for an approaching airplane. Other distinctive floral traits of the orchid family are that all of the reproductive parts are fused into a single structure called the column and the pollen has become a solid fused mass—not the familiar dust-like pollen of other plants. These remarkable flowers exist in every color and hue of the rainbow and an endless variety of shapes and form. To our eye the blooms can be beautiful or bizarre, even looking more animal than plant, with some resembling birds, butterflies, or spiders.

Orchids have evolved complex relationships with many types of pollinators, including hummingbirds, crickets, night-flying moths, and a wide variety of other insects. Some flowers are masters of deception, offering up fake promises of nectar or food, in some cases even mimicking other non-orchid species of plants. The most lurid orchid-pollinator relationships are those in which the orchids produce flowers that resemble female insects in order to deceive the males into mating with the blooms to achieve pollination. Fragrance also plays an important role in pollination, and many orchids have evolved strong and complex fragrances to accompany their blooms. Some are subtle and delicate, producing only faint fragrances, whereas others can perfume an entire room with their scent. Orchids can smell like roses, jasmine, hyacinth, coconut, banana, and other sweet fragrances. Other orchids that are pollinated by flies can smell quite rotten, rancid, or sour.

ORCHID HABITATS AND ANATOMY

Basic knowledge of the anatomy of an orchid, the different growth forms, and how the plants absorb water and nutrients is essential for understanding how to care for an orchid compared to another houseplant. The proper techniques for watering, feeding, repotting, and dividing plants are developed based on the natural habitat and anatomy of the orchid plant.

FŪKIRAN

Some cultures have built their appreciation of orchid foliage and form, rather than the flowers themselves. In Japan and China, many of their native orchids are grown for their variations in foliage, with collectors seeking out variegated, contorted, or unusually shaped and twisted foliage. The simple grace and appearance of the narrow foliage of cymbidiums has been a popular motif in decorative arts and painting for thousands of years.

One of the most popular of traditional Japanese orchids in cultivation is *Vanda falcata* (formerly *Neofinetia falcata*), traditionally known as *furan* or *Fūkiran*. At one time in history, this prized orchid was collected and cultivated only by nobility, with the plants treated, admired, and displayed like fine art more than a garden subject. Fūkiran plants are displayed in beautifully crafted and decorated pottery and even protected by woven gilded cages, all part of the traditional display to highlight the beauty of the plant's form. There has been a recent resurgence in interest in the traditional cultivation and display of these prized orchid plants, with Fūkiran societies growing in membership around the world.

Vanda falcata is still grown and appreciated in its native Japan for the beauty and variation of the foliage as much as the delicate and sweetly scented flowers.

Orchid plants can be found as terrestrials growing in the ground or as epiphytes growing in the canopy of trees. The majority of orchids that are grown in the home are actually tropical epiphytes. These orchids have evolved the ability to grow attached to the branches or trunk of their host plant with specialized roots, stems, and leaves that allow them to grow and thrive without soil. Epiphytes are not parasites and do not harm their host trees, but take advantage of the additional light, air movement, moisture, and space in the canopy without much competition from other plants. Orchids are not the only epiphytes, and many plant families have adapted to life in the canopy, such as bromeliads, ferns, aroids, and even some cacti.

Orchids can be divided into two groups based on their growth habits: either monopodial or sympodial. Monopodial orchids grow from one stem point upward and produce leaves, roots, and flowers from a vertical stem. Examples of monopodial orchids include *Phalaenopsis* and *Vanda*, which produce alternating leaves along a central stem. Most other orchid genera, including *Cattleya, Oncidium, Cymbidium*, and *Dendrobium*, are sympodial orchids in which multiple stems are produced along a creeping stem called a rhizome. These thickened rhizomes grow along the ground or tree surface and can produce multiple new growth points from a single lead growth. Over time, they form large clumps that grow in many different directions. The roots of sympodial orchids are produced at the base of the growth along the rhizome. Knowing the growth type of an orchid is important for understanding the best way to divide, repot, or propagate a particular plant.

The stems of many sympodial orchids are swollen into structures called pseudobulbs. Although they resemble the underground bulb of a tulip or onion,

By growing attached to branches and trunks of trees, this *Dendrobium aemulum* orchid can take advantage of the best available light, air movement, and space in the forest canopy.

pseudobulbs have completely different structures. The aboveground pseudobulbs of an orchid are more like the modified stems of a cactus, which allow the plants to store nutrients and water between periods of rain. Pseudobulbs vary in shape and size. Some are long and narrow and resemble bamboo, like those of *Dendrobium*, whereas others are short and rounded, like those of *Oncidium*. Monopodial orchids lack pseudobulbs and instead utilize their roots and thickened leaves for water storage rather than their stems.

The roots of orchids are also specialized for their unusual growth habits. Orchid roots are thickened and often silvery white. They are covered with a spongy layer called velamen, which is adapted for the quick absorption of water and nutrients in their epiphytic environment. The active growing tip of the root is often

Monopodial orchids, like this *Vanda*, grow upward from a single point and add new leaves above the old ones on an elongating stem.

The swollen bulb-like stems of orchids, called pseudobulbs, are adapted to store water and nutrients for growth.

bright green, and as the root expands it can help attach the plant securely to any surface—whether the vertical branch of a tree, the potting medium, or the pot the plant is growing in. Orchid plants do not produce dense networks of fibrous roots like some plants do. Some orchid species can fill a pot with roots, whereas others produce small masses of thickened roots that support the entire orchid plant.

JEWEL ORCHIDS

There's a whole world of orchids that are celebrated by collectors for their colored and shimmering foliage rather than their blooms. Known as jewel orchids for the remarkable patterns and sparkling foliage, they are an easy-to-grow, very collectable, and beautiful group of plants. These terrestrial orchids are found throughout the world in shaded forests in both temperate and tropical regions. They evolved foliage patterns as a means of camouflage on the forest floor, resembling fallen leaves or deceiving herbivores into thinking they are inedible or unpalatable. On closer examination, these adaptations are startling in their complexity and beauty. Leaves with networks of golden veins, deep velvet textures, glittering surfaces, and contrasting spots and lines are just some of the patterns that make jewel orchids delightful horticultural subjects.

The more popular jewel orchids, such as *Ludisia, Macodes*, and *Anoectochilus*, have dark green or purple velvet-textured leaves overlaid with reticulated patterns of red and gold veins that sparkle whenever light hits their surface. The popularity of *Ludisia discolor* is increasing, even among non-orchid growers, for the beautiful foliage and ease of culture.

Many of the plants have small green, white, or yellow flowers with a subtle beauty. Collectors often pinch off developing flowers to increase the amount of foliage the plants produce. However, a few jewel orchids produce attractive spikes flowers, such as the flaming red spires of *Spiranthes speciosa*. The tall spikes of emerald green serpentine flowers of *Sarcoglottis* are an added bonus to the plants' silver spotted or barred foliage.

TOP *Goodyera pubescens* is an evergreen jewel orchid native to the forests of eastern North America.

ABOVE Jewel orchids are prized for the varied textures, colors, and intricate patterns of their foliage.

WILD ORCHID
Conservation

The desire for orchids has put a terrible pressure on wild plant populations. Since Victorian times, orchids have been gathered around the world by the millions and sold to collectors captivated by the lure of such beautiful blooms. Vast forests once supplied a seemingly endless number and variety of plants for harvest to feed the public demand for exotic orchids. We now know, however, that orchids reproduce slowly, are found in specialized environments, and often have very limited geographic distributions, with some species only being known from a single locale. The native forests and other habitats of these prized plants are rapidly disappearing due to logging, agriculture, and expanding human settlements, in addition to the continued collection of wild plants for the orchid market. The future of many tropical plants seems grim in the face of these many threats, as well as habitat loss caused by climate change.

Forests are being cut down at alarming rates to provide food and other resources for growing human populations, in turn destroying the habitats essential for many orchids.

There are national and international laws in place to protect orchid species. Unfortunately, laws don't stop some people from collecting plants and selling them to make a quick profit. Conservationists, botanical gardens, botanists, and horticulturists are working together to conserve wild plant populations in nature preserves and propagate species to help reduce the pressure for wild-collected plants. Through these efforts, several orchid species have been saved from the brink of extinction, including *Paphiopedilum vietnamense*, which was recently discovered in Thai Nguyen Province in Vietnam.

Orchid conservation should be part of any serious orchid grower's perspective. Every effort should be made to purchase plants that come from reputable orchid nurseries that propagate their plants rather than collect them from the wild. Plants should not be removed from the wild, no matter how tempting it might be. More often than not, wild-collected plants take a long time to adapt and survive in cultivated conditions. Nursery-propagated plants are also more vigorous and grow and perform better than their wild counterparts.

ORCHID NAMES

To a novice, orchid growers seem to have their own language full of abbreviations, complex botanical names, and a lingo that's difficult to understand. And sometimes the names of orchids change, making it challenging to keep up with the proper terminology. *Brassavola digbyana* is now *Rhyncholaelia digbyana*? Some members of *Laelia* are now classified as *Cattleya*, while others still belong to *Laelia*? What's the difference between *Odontobrassia* and *Miltassia* orchids? What do the abbreviations *Bc.* and *Rlc.* mean, and is it relevant to my plant? Other orchid growers keep talking about their "cats" and "dens." What does that mean? Even trying to read an orchid label can make you feel like you need a decoder ring to decipher what all those letters and words mean. Once you get the hang of it, though, it's not that difficult.

The complex names of orchids are created to help growers understand the origin, history, and pedigree of their plants. A little terminology will help you understand what that jumble of words on the label really means.

GENUS

A genus is a natural grouping of related species that share similar characteristics, such as *Cattleya* or *Vanda*. A genus can contain from one to several thousand different species. Horticulturists have also devised genus names for hybrid orchids that are crosses of natural genera that grow in the wild. For example *Brassocattleya* orchids are crosses of *Brassavola* and *Cattleya* and *Aliceara* orchids are crosses of *Brassia, Miltonia*, and *Oncidium*.

SPECIES

A species is a naturally occurring plant that grows in the wild, and these are assigned a Latin binomial by botanists, such as *Brassavola nodosa* or *Paphiopedilum delenatii*. The first letter of the genus name is capitalized and the species epithet is lowercase. Species names are usually written in italics to indicate they are natural species and not manmade hybrids.

HYBRID

Although natural hybrids do occur, the majority of orchid hybrids are created by artificially breeding two different varieties. Hybrids can be made between species or existing hybrids or any combination of related plants. More than 100,000 orchid hybrids have been created, and the number grows by the thousands each year. Breeders give hybrids a variety name, which follows the genus name, such as *Cattleya* Mini Purple and *Aliceara* Marfitch. If a hybrid has not been formally named, an

The hybrid genus *Aliceara* was created by crossing three natural orchid genera.

The species *Cattleya maxima* grows naturally in dry forests of Venezuela and Peru.

× symbol is written between the two parents' names to indicate the hybrid, such as *Vanda* Princess Mikasa × Robert's Delight.

CULTIVAR

Orchid breeders often select a particular plant of a species or hybrid for an exceptional quality, such as a distinctive flower color or leaf variegation, compared to others of similar type. That particular plant is then assigned a cultivar name, which is placed in single quotation marks, such as *Cymbidium* Sara Jean 'Ice Cascade' or *Paphiopedilum* Maudiae 'Magnificum'. The cultivar name is sometimes referred to as the clonal name, as these plants are multiplied, always retaining that cultivar name for that unique plant.

AWARD

Many orchid plants also have a series of letters after the cultivar name, such as HCC/AOS, AM/AOS, or AM/JOGA. These letters represent awards bestowed upon the cultivar in recognition of their exceptional quality or rarity. Organizations such as the American Orchid Society (AOS) or the Japan Orchid Growers Association (JOGA) have orchid shows where highly trained judges evaluate plants. If they meet certain criteria, the plants can receive individual awards, such as a Highly Commendable Certificate (HCC) or an Award of Merit (AM) among other awards.

Most orchid growers use abbreviations as common written and spoken shorthand for long genus names. Growers commonly refer to *Phalaenopsis* orchids as "phals" or *Paphiopedilum* orchids as "paphs." All orchid genera have assigned abbreviations, making it easier to write out long orchid names. Some common abbreviations include:

Alcra.	*Aliceara*
Ang.	*Angraecum*
Bc.	*Brassocattleya*
C.	*Cattleya*
Cym.	*Cymbidium*
Den.	*Dendrobium*
Epi.	*Epidendrum*
Milt.	*Miltonia*
Onc.	*Oncidium*
Paph.	*Paphiopedilum*
Phal.	*Phalaenopsis*
Phrag.	*Phragmipedium*
Rlc.	*Rhyncholaeilocattleya*
Tol.	*Tolumnia*
V.	*Vanda*

NAME CHANGES

Historically, all epiphytic orchids were placed in the genus *Epidendrum* from the Greek *epi* meaning "upon" and *dendron* meaning "tree." As more orchids were discovered and named by scientists, they began to further understand and catalog orchid diversity, where the plants originated, and how they possibly evolved. In the past several decades, scientists have begun to analyze and compare the DNA of orchid species and understand more deeply the evolution and family tree of the orchid family. We now have a much clearer picture of which plants are close relatives to others and, more specifically, how closely related they are.

Plants once thought to be distant relatives are now classified within the same genus, causing a flurry of name changes for familiar plants—and, as an unintended result, causing frustrated horticulturists to have to learn new names and correct the labels in their pots. Whether you choose to use the new name or an older name, most orchid growers will understand which plant you're speaking about. Many references and nurseries still use the older names for orchids, and you might see the same orchid species listed under more than one genus name.

Orchids make excellent houseplants and adapt well to the conditions found in our homes.

Keeping ORCHIDS *Happy and Healthy*

—»‹‹—

GROWING ORCHIDS IN THE HOME can be a rewarding and engaging hobby. Whether you're looking to learn proper care for one plant or to start building a collection of plants, orchids are full of opportunities no matter what your style or level of experience. Orchids are adaptable, long-lived, and floriferous houseplants when provided with the right conditions and care. Despite their undeserved reputation of being fussy, orchids are actually much easier to grow than most people believe.

Many orchids grow happily in the same conditions we find comfortable in our own homes. By selecting the right plant for the right location, you will not have to modify or change your environment to suit a particular plant. Choose the orchids that like you, rather than the orchids you like.

A simple bit of observation of the growing conditions in your home can get you off to a good start and avoid disappointment later. Different locations have various amounts of sunlight and humidity and different temperatures throughout the day, and these conditions can change dramatically throughout the year. Matching your home's growing conditions with the right kind of orchid is the first part of the formula for success.

In order to understand what conditions the plant will experience, ask yourself the following six questions.

Does the location have natural sunlight?
How strong is the sunlight?
How long does the location receive natural light each day?
What temperatures will there be throughout the year? In the daytime?
  At night?

Is the air constantly dry or does it have some moisture?
How often will I water and care for the plants?

That last question is difficult, but it's important to be honest with yourself.

Not all locations are suitable for growing orchids, and others can become so with a little creativity and simple modification. By combining knowledge of how most orchids grow in the wild with an understanding of the location's conditions, you can start to create the ideal place for orchids to thrive. One of the best ways to do that is to replicate an orchid's natural environment in the unnatural conditions of your home. You don't need to re-create a tropical rainforest in your living room to provide the basic needs of an orchid, you just need to make some slight modifications in potting and provide the right amounts of light, humidity, and food.

If we were to imagine ourselves as an epiphytic orchid growing on a branch in the tropics, what would we experience? Light as bright dappled sunlight filtered through the canopy of the tree. Air movement would be generous and buoyant. Water provided by tropical rains would be regular and copious but with periods of drying out between storms. Drainage would be rapid, allowing water to run off quickly and air to circulate around the roots. The level of humidity in the rainforest would be constant and relatively high. Nutrients would be provided in small amounts from the layer of mosses and the branches of the host tree. With the right combination of materials and simple techniques, we can provide similar light, air, water, humidity, and nutrients as an orchid experiences in the wild.

LIGHT LEVELS AND PLACEMENT

Light is one of the most important qualities in choosing the right location for orchids in your home. Proper light is necessary for the plant to photosynthesize and make the food it needs to develop and grow. Depending on the direction that the window faces, light intensity varies greatly and even changes from season to season. Locations with southern or western exposures have some of the strongest light intensities, whereas a northern exposure will be shaded and darker throughout the entire day. An east-facing windowsill is among the best locations for proper light intensity without being overpowering during the highest temperatures of the day.

Light requirements for orchids can vary greatly, even within the same genus, depending on the natural habitat and breeding. Understanding the conditions in your home will help you choose the right orchid for those light levels. If you have only low light conditions, the addition of a grow light can help orchids get the light they need. Most orchids require at least 6 hours of light each day to grow and bloom well. If a plant is not blooming, try slowly increasing the amount of light

CURATING
an Orchid Collection

Many people collect, grow, and exhibit orchids they've acquired over many years, while sharing divisions with friends and hunting down rare and unusual plants. With the enormous variety of plants available, many orchid growers choose to focus their collections around a cohesive theme. Here are several ideas for developing a collection.

Type or genus: One of the more common themes is to build a collection around a single type, such as slipper orchids, or genus, such as *Cattleya* hybrids. These collections often reflect a grower's favorite orchids or a group of plants that grow particularly well in certain conditions.

Species: Some orchid growers appreciate naturally occurring species over manmade hybrids. The array of species available to the hobbyist is extremely diverse and full of choices for every taste and growing condition. You can specialize in species of a particular genus or even just a single species and its natural variations.

Antique and heirloom: Orchid hybridizing has been practiced for more than 200 years. Many of these hybrids and their original plants still exist in collections today. These older plants represent the living history of orchid growing and breeding, telling stories of famous collectors, breeders, and orchid nurseries long gone.

Miniatures: If you have limited space, miniature orchids are an excellent way to build a diverse and interesting collection of plants. The world of miniatures offers a wonderful range of plants for orchid collectors who appreciate the delicate beauty of these compact plants. And there are miniature equivalents of just about every standard type of orchid to be found.

Geographic locale: With orchids growing naturally throughout the world, you can even choose to collect orchids of a particular region or country. A collection of species or hybrids is a great way to connect with your heritage, a culture, or geographic region that interests you.

For those with limited space for larger plants, miniature orchids can provide a wide range of blooms just as beautiful as their larger cousins.

Paphiopedilum Julius 'Kiaora' will grow and bloom in lower light conditions.

it receives. By gradually moving the plant over several weeks closer to a brighter location, it will prevent the leaves from burning with the sudden change in sunlight.

The best way to measure whether an orchid is receiving the proper amount of sunlight is by looking at the growth of the plant. The leaves should be a bright light green, and the leaves, new growth, and pseudobulbs should be upright and strong—not floppy. Dark green leaves can be the sign of a lack of sunlight needed by the plant. If a plant is receiving too much sunlight, leaves will become yellowish green and even nearly white if bleached by the sun. In strong light conditions, the leaves of many orchids blush with reddish purple pigments as a means of protection against the sun. Direct intense sunlight can quickly burn soft-leaved plants such as *Phalaenopsis*. Once the leaves have browned, there is no way to repair them. New leaves will have to grow for the plant to continue to survive.

As the seasons progress, light intensity changes and the position of the strongest rays move. Watch your plants' foliage closely, especially as the low light of winter changes to spring and eventually summer, when light intensity increases dramatically. A windowsill that was ideal in January can become hazardous in June, as orchids can burn in several hours of direct hot sun. Placing a sheer curtain between the plants and the window or setting them back further will moderate the damaging powers of unobstructed light.

Orchids for strong light	Orchids for medium light	Orchids for low light
Cattleya	*Miltoniopsis*	jewel orchids
Cymbidium	*Oncidium*	*Masdevallia*
Dendrobium	*Phaius*	*Paphiopedilum*
Tolumnia	*Phragmipedium*	*Phalaenopsis*
Vanda		

If a windowsill with natural sunlight is unavailable, many types of orchids will grow and bloom to perfection under artificial lights.

GROWING ORCHIDS UNDER ARTIFICIAL LIGHTS

Many home gardeners believe that the dream of growing such beautiful flowers is lost since they don't have a sunny windowsill or a greenhouse to cultivate a collection of orchids. In fact, growing orchids under artificial lights indoors can be even easier than battling with shady windows, limited sunlight, or not enough windowsill space for plants to grow well. Growing orchids under lights doesn't require a huge investment in technology either, with many plants growing and blooming well under simple inexpensive fixtures rather than expensive high-energy grow lights. A room full of thriving and blooming orchid plants where you thought it could never happen will easily overcome the doubts about such an investment.

Artificial lights can be added to existing windows to help supplement light during darker winter weather or to compensate for shaded or blocked light that prevents plants from growing well. Many orchid growers have overcome their space limitations by converting a spare room or basements into a growing space where orchids thrive despite having no natural sunlight. There's a wealth of options for lighting fixtures on the market, with fluorescent, high-intensity discharge (HID), and light-emitting diode (LED) fixtures being the three most common used by home orchid growers. Each type has pros and cons for their use, their energy consumption, and how well the plants grow. When choosing between lighting options, look for bulbs that produce full-spectrum light in order to provide plants with the necessary wavelengths of light they need for the best growth and flowering.

Fluorescent lights are the most popular and the most easily available of all of the types of lighting. The light produced by fluorescent fixtures is relatively soft and not as intense as other bulbs. Simple 4-foot fluorescent shop lights can be used, with two fixtures (four bulbs) being able to provide enough light for the majority of orchids to grow and bloom well. Start with a minimum of 40 watt bulbs for low-light varieties such as *Paphiopedilum* and *Phalaenopsis* and a minimum of 60 watt bulbs for orchids that prefer brighter light. If you cannot find full-spectrum bulbs, a mix of cool white and warm white bulbs will provide the full spectrum of light needed for plant growth. Fluorescent bulbs produce the brightest light and greatest output toward the center, so place plants needing stronger light toward the center and low-light plants toward the ends of the lights. Place the fixture about 6 to 8 inches from the tops of the leaves and not further than 12 inches above the foliage. Because fluorescent light is not as intense as natural sunlight, the plants should receive 12 to 14 hours of light each day to ensure they have enough light to grow and bloom well. Some growers increase the light to 14 to 16 hours during the summer months to simulate a change in the seasons for the plants and stimulate blooming for some types of orchids. Fluorescent bulbs slowly dim over time and should be replaced every 2 years; although this isn't noticeable to our eyes, the plants won't grow as well if the bulbs are not replaced regularly.

Among artificial lights, HIDs are some of the most intense and come closest to replicating natural sunlight. Although this technology was created for the indoor gardener, HIDs are still a comparatively expensive option both in terms of initial cost and energy consumption. They are intense enough for high-light orchids such as *Vanda* and *Cattleya* to do well and can be placed several feet above the plants, with one fixture illuminating many plants. HIDs produce light in the yellow–orange spectrum and because of their strong output can generate considerable amounts of heat. They require a little more detailed understanding of growing under lights and proper measurement of light intensity, and so are best used by the more advanced grower.

LEDs are a relatively recent addition to home orchid growing, as the cost of this lighting technology has come down considerably in recent years. These lights are often structured to look like fluorescent fixtures and can be used instead to improve energy efficiency and increase light intensity. There are even LED options designed to replace fluorescent bulbs, so you don't have to change your fixtures. Unlike fluorescent bulbs, LEDs do not have the problem of decreased light intensity toward the ends and provide more even light throughout the growing space. However, the intensity of LED fixtures is much greater than that of fluorescent bulbs, which allows the fixtures to be placed at a greater distance from the plants. If the LEDs are placed too close, they will burn the plants not due to the temperature but the intensity of the light they produce. When choosing an LED fixture, look for a full-spectrum option or one that has a minimum light temperature of 4000K to provide the light spectrum that orchids need to grow.

WATER QUALITY AND HUMIDITY

Proper watering is the most important skill and perhaps the most critical variable in growing orchids in the home. Water plays several important roles for plant growth and health. Most importantly, water absorbed through the roots is necessary for an orchid's survival, growth, and flowering. Water is also the source of nutrients for the plant. Water allows roots to draw these required nutrients up into the body of the plant, where they are stored and utilized for growth and flowering.

Many orchids are epiphytes, and they are sometimes incorrectly referred to as air plants. However, they cannot extract all the water they require from the surrounding atmosphere. They need water applied in and around the roots to survive. The process of watering also provides oxygen to the roots and container. As water flows through the pot, it carries oxygen to the root system. As water drains out of the bottom of the container, air is pulled down into the potting medium and provides additional aeration. A stagnant root system with too much water and not enough air encourages certain types of pathogens, suffocates the roots of the plant, and eventually causes the plant to decline and die. Water flowing through the open potting medium also flushes out any accumulated fertilizer, minerals, and decomposed potting medium and even helps to reduce pests and diseases around the roots.

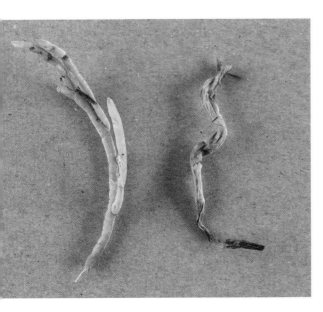

Live and healthy roots (left) are silvery white or light green and are firm to the touch, whereas dead or decaying roots (right) are brown, papery, or soft and often hollow.

One of the best methods for watering an orchid is to take the plant to the sink and allow water to flow freely through the potting mix and out of drainage holes on the bottom of the pot. Small volumes of water provide moisture for the roots but will not aerate and flush out the potting medium. Submerging the plant is not ideal because many potting mixes float out of the container, which may displace the growing plant. Similarly, sitting the pot partially or completely in water can drown roots if left too long and may transfer diseases from one plant to another. Allowing the water to flow throughout the container for a few seconds, letting the water drain, and repeating the process two to three times is all that an orchid needs.

When watering the plants, use tepid water since many orchids are sensitive to water temperature. Cold water can damage leaves

Allowing water to flow freely through the container provides the proper amount and helps to aerate and saturate the potting medium, which is beneficial to the root system.

and roots, spotting them and even killing plant cells if the water is cold enough. Epiphytic orchids are tropical plants and are not adapted to cold showers. Hot water can have the same damaging effect on the plants' leaves and roots.

Watering is best done in the morning to allow the orchid's leaves and growth to dry before nightfall. Wet leaves and water in the new growth or crowns of plants can encourage disease, and allowing the plants to dry before nightfall is a simple way to prevent certain types of rot and fungus from attacking plants. Water quality can be important for some orchids, and using water low in minerals is best for orchid plants.

Deciding when to water plants is not solved with a simple formula for success such as "water orchids twice a week." When a plant needs to be watered will vary depending on the potting medium, container choice, season, temperature, type of orchid, and even flowering. Many orchids have pseudobulbs that allow the plant to store water, and plants such as *Cattleya, Dendrobium, Cymbidium,* and *Oncidium* orchids can be allowed to approach dryness between watering. Orchids without water storage organs, such as *Paphiopedilum, Phragmipedium,* and *Vanda,* should be kept evenly moist without drying out for long periods.

Remember that your home's growing environment is unique, and no two locations have exactly the same conditions. By observing your orchids over time, you will begin to notice the subtle clues that tell you everything you need to know about when and how much water they need. Here are some simple things you can do to hone your watering skills.

- Plants require more water in hot weather than in cooler weather. Higher temperatures will mean more evaporation and water needed to keep the plants hydrated.
- Check the container for signs of moisture. Look at the drainage holes and see if the potting medium is wet or dry. Feel the outside of the container; terra cotta or other porous containers will feel moist and cool to the touch, letting you know that there is still moisture in the pot.
- Feel the weight of the pot. Is it heavy or light? A recently watered container will be much heavier than one that has dried out completely. Feel the weight of each pot as you water, and in time you'll be able to tell when a plant needs water just by lifting the pot.
- Place a small bamboo or wood skewer or even a pencil into the pot along the edge as far down as it will go and leave it in place. To see if there is moisture in the container, remove the stick. If it is dry to the touch, it is likely to be a good time to water the plant.

- If in doubt, hold off on watering the plant for another day or so and check it again. You can always increase the amount of water for another day, but it is virtually impossible to take water away once you add it. Overwatering is probably the most common cause of failure with orchids.

MAINTAINING HUMIDITY AND AIR CIRCULATION

The greatest diversity of orchids grows in humid regions of the tropics. Their epiphytic lifestyle and their physiology are adapted to growing in areas where there is abundant ambient moisture from cloud forests and frequent rains. Although humidity is high, the air around the plants is not stagnant. Orchids grow in areas where moving air currents occur, creating a buoyant atmosphere around the plants.

Humidity is water vapor in the air, and you cannot compensate for a lack of humidity by providing the roots with more water. During winter months, humidity in a home with the heat running can drop to as low as 20%, which can easily damage and dehydrate plants. Some plants are more tolerant of low humidity than others and the ability to grow and bloom properly under such conditions will vary. Humidity and air circulation are linked together in the growing environment and both must be provided. Combined together they create ideal conditions, but one without the other becomes problematic for orchid plants.

Ideally, orchids grow best when provided with a minimum of 45–50% humidity. To accurately measure humidity, purchase an inexpensive humidistat and place it near the plants. Many growers use the technique of placing the plants on water trays filled with pebbles to aid the evaporation of water. The pots should sit above the layer of water and gravel and not with the bottoms resting in the reservoir of water. As water evaporates, it helps to increase the humidity around the plants. Running a small ultrasonic humidifier also can protect plants from the drying effects of heating a home in winter or arid climates. Misting plants with a hand sprayer only increases the humidity around the plants temporarily and will not combat the lack of humidify in a dry room. Placing orchids near other plants and grouping them together also helps to create a humid microclimate, a localized area of higher humidity around the plants. Water vapor naturally released into the air by groups of plants increases the humidity and will benefit all of your plants, not just the orchids.

In the canopy of humid tropical forests where epiphytic orchids originate, the atmosphere is always moving via natural convection and from passing rainstorms. The air movement does not have to be strong, just enough to keep the environment from becoming stagnant. Providing air circulation is also an initial line of defense

Placing plants in a tray filled with gravel and water helps moisture to evaporate and provides additional ambient humidity for the growing plants.

to help prevent several pest and disease issues, including bacterial and fungal rots, leaf spotting, and certain insect pests. Moving air and air exchange around plants help them to get the proper carbon dioxide and oxygen concentrations needed for photosynthesis and respiration and remove any buildup of gasses like ethylene that can contribute to buds dropping before they open. In warmer weather, circulating air helps to cool foliage and dry off leaf surfaces, which improves the overall health and growth of the plants.

Improving air circulation around plants can mean spacing them out slightly to prevent overcrowded and cramped conditions and allowing air to move around all sides of the plant. When the temperatures and weather allow, you can also crack a window nearby to provide fresh air for the plants. Placing a small fan in the growing area can help, especially where plants are crowded and growing densely together. The fan should be near the plants but not pointed directly at them to prevent the moving air from drying out the leaves and roots too much, which can desiccate the plants if the humidity is low.

TEMPERATURE

Considering the diversity and distribution of the orchid family from hot tropical rainforests to cool high-altitude cloud forests, the temperatures that each type of orchid will thrive in depends on where it grows naturally. To simplify the range of temperatures and environments that orchids are found in, orchid growers classify plants as either warm, intermediate, or cool growers based on their optimal temperature ranges.

Temperature is also important to trigger flowering in many plants. Most orchids require a fluctuation between day and night temperatures of at least 10°F to grow and bloom successfully. Plants will bloom better with this drop in temperature, especially in spring and fall.

The air temperature of the growing environment can be monitored with a simple thermometer placed among the plants and out of direct sunlight. Rather than guess, it is best to get an accurate temperature measurement to ensure that the plants are receiving the right conditions to bloom, as even a difference of 3–5°F can disrupt blooming for some varieties of orchids. The leaf temperature should be monitored as well; the best method is simply feeling the foliage and making sure it's not hot to the touch. Plants can easily overheat in hot weather, especially when very dry at the roots. Water evaporating through the pores in the leaves will help

Temperature group	Ideal temperature range	Day temperatures	Night temperatures
Warm growers	60–90°F	72–85°F; can tolerate temperatures above 90°F	65–70°F; minimum of 55°F preferred
Intermediate growers	55–85°F	70–80°F; temperatures below 85°F best	50–65°F
Cool growers	50–80°F	65–75°F; should not exceed 85°F for long periods	50–55°F

cool a plant during hot weather, so it's important to keep plants properly hydrated during hot weather. As the leaf temperature increases, the foliage can burn from the combination of high light levels and air temperatures.

FEEDING

Like all plants, orchids require nutrients to grow, flower, and reproduce. Despite the fact that plants manufacture their food from sunlight by photosynthesis—or the false assumption that orchids are "air plants" and somehow absorb all they need from the surrounding atmosphere—orchids still need food. As gardeners, we provide food for our plants by applying fertilizer. It is true that the potting medium can provide some nutrients, but what's contained in the limited volume is not enough for the plant to survive and thrive for the long term. In nature, nutrients are provided through several biological and chemical processes in the atmosphere and at the root zone of the plant. When we cultivate plants indoors, however, they cannot access these natural processes and must be fed.

There are two main types of fertilizer that we can use to feed orchids. Inorganic fertilizers are scientifically formulated from synthetic nutrients and other minerals to provide complete nutrition for growing plants, whereas organic fertilizers are derived from natural materials. Fertilizers can either be used as liquids watered into the plants or as slow-release pellets, granules, or powders applied as top dressings to containers.

PLANT NUTRITION

All plants require a certain set of nutrients for their proper growth and flowering. Each nutrient plays an important role in the plant, helping with cell maintenance, growth, photosynthesis, or flowering. They can be divided into two groups: macronutrients, which are needed in larger quantities, and micronutrients, which are still required but in lesser amounts for proper plant health.

The macronutrients include nitrogen, phosphorus, and potassium.

Nitrogen (N) is the most important macronutrient because it plays a role in plant growth, photosynthesis, and flowering. A lack of nitrogen causes yellowing and may slow or stunt plant growth. The amount of nitrogen provided can also limit and control how other nutrients are absorbed and utilized, controlling the overall growth of the plant.

Phosphorous (P) plays an important role in photosynthesis. Phosphorous also encourages cell growth and development and root and shoot growth, and it helps plants store energy.

Potassium (K) is involved in plant metabolism. Its function is important in regulating water and nutrient transport in and out of cells and is necessary for many adaptations to the growing environment. Potassium is also involved in the opening and closing of the leaf pores that allow the plant to photosynthesize and breathe.

The micronutrients include iron (Fe), manganese (Mn), boron (B), and several others that are needed in only small amounts for plant growth. Most complete fertilizers contain the necessary micronutrients. If orchid plants are fed regularly, there is little danger of them lacking the needed supply.

INORGANIC FERTILIZERS

Inorganic or chemical fertilizers are the standard fertilizers used by both amateur and commercial orchid growers. Most are sold as a water-soluble solid or as liquid concentrate that is mixed and applied to the plant during watering. Several different formulations are available, and they vary in their percentages of micro- and macronutrients, with some fertilizers designed for specific purposes or types of plants. Inorganic fertilizers are easy to apply, and because of the greater concentration of nutrients than found in organic fertilizers, they often provide the best results in stimulating growth and flowering.

ORGANIC FERTILIZERS

Organic fertilizers are created from a diverse range of natural materials from fish and seaweed emulsions to ground bone and blood meal to compost and manure teas. Many organic fertilizers are not in a form that makes the nutrients immediately available to the plant. Instead, they require some biological and chemical processes to break them down further so the plant can access and use them. In addition, organic fertilizers contain relatively weak concentrations of macro- and micronutrients. Many growers supplement applications of inorganic fertilizers with fish and seaweed emulsions to provide more than one type of nutrient source for their plants, and they describe much better growth and rooting for some kinds of orchids, such as vandas and cattleyas. Organic fertilizers can be either dissolved in water or provided in solid forms such as granules or powders applied to the roots. One of the main drawbacks of organic fertilizers is that their composition causes a noticeable odor, and when using a product like fish emulsion the strong "low tide" smell can be unpleasant, especially in closed areas. Although the odors are disagreeable to many people, they will dissipate over time and with ventilation.

SLOW-RELEASE FERTILIZERS

Slow-release fertilizers are pellets or small spherical prills designed to release nutrients slowly over a period of time. While seemingly convenient and making feeding easier, most of these products are designed for plants that are grown in soil and that require more nutrients than most orchids need. Many of these fertilizers can be quite variable in the amount of fertilizer they release over time and at different temperatures. When growing orchids, slow-release fertilizers should be used sparingly because they can burn the sensitive roots of orchids with too much fertilizer and the excess nutrients can speed the breakdown of potting medium. Although some orchid growers use them with excellent results, it is best to have more control over how much and how often you feed your plants than these products allow.

HOW TO FEED ORCHID PLANTS

Deciding when and how to fertilize your plants does not have to be a complex operation, and reading and understanding fertilizer labels doesn't require a chemistry degree. Fertilizers are classified by the basic macronutrient composition, which is represented by a three-number formula on the label. The first number corresponds with the percentage of nitrogen (N), the second phosphorous (P), and the third potassium (K). The label will also list any micronutrients that are present in the formulation.

An inorganic liquid fertilizer is the most common and perhaps the easiest way to control the amount of nutrients orchid plants receive. Traditionally, a fertilizer high in nitrogen (30-10-10) was recommended for orchids, because the bark potting medium that most plants were potted in was believed to become nitrogen deficient over time. Growers then alternated or supplemented with a so-called blossom booster fertilizer (10-30-20) to encourage the plants to flower. Nowadays, however, most growers have simplified the feeding process by using a more complete balanced fertilizer, one in which all three numbers are the same or similar (20-20-20, 20-10-20, or 14-14-14), while making sure that micronutrients are included in the formula as well.

Because orchids do not receive large amounts of food naturally, the nutrient concentrations applied to the plant do not have to be very high. In fact, it's much better for the health of the plant to apply low concentrations of fertilizer frequently than larger amounts intermittently. The vast majority of orchids are tropical plants that grow year-round, so consistent regular feedings also result in much more robust growth and flowering. Many orchid growers follow the adage "weekly weakly" when it comes to feeding plants. A balanced fertilizer applied at one-quarter strength every third to fourth watering should be sufficient for the proper feeding of most orchids.

Too much of a good thing can become a problem, and many orchids when fed too much, especially with high-nitrogen fertilizers, can become robust dark green specimens that are reluctant to bloom. When applied at higher concentrations, fertilizer can build up in the potting medium, which encourages the medium to break down quickly and can burn the sensitive roots of plants. Occasional flushing of the pot with clean water can help to prevent the buildup of fertilizer salts in the potting medium.

POTS AND BASKETS

A diverse range of container options is available to the home orchid grower. Plastic, clay, ceramic, and specially designed orchid pots and baskets can be purchased in every size, color, and shape imaginable.

When choosing a container, select something that will allow for 1 to 2 years of growth for the plant. Due to the nature of their roots, most orchids prefer to be snug rather than potted in containers with too much extra space. Some growers believe that if the roots are potted tightly it will actually cause the plants to produce more shoots, leaves, and flowers than a plant with ample room for the roots to wander through a container. It's also easier to monitor moisture levels and watering in a smaller container versus a larger one.

PLASTIC POTS

Over the years, plastic pots have come a long way in their design and engineering. Plastic pots are being created with improved drainage, and some are almost indistinguishable from terra cotta and other more decorative materials.

Orchids grow very well in plastic containers provided that they have suitable drainage. Look for pots that have several drainage holes at the bottom to allow for the mix to drain freely when watering. Since plastic is not porous, plants grown in these pots tend to hold moisture for longer periods between watering. Plastic pots are lightweight and easily cleaned and sterilized. Some disadvantages are that over time they can become brittle and have a much shorter lifespan than other containers, but they are inexpensive enough that they can be replaced and recycled once they are no longer useable.

TO CUT
or Not to Cut?

Once the flowers of an orchid plant have faded, the blooms shrivel and drop off, leaving a bare green flower spike. After blooming, most orchids produce new growth, roots, and stems, getting larger and preparing for next year's flowering. You might wonder what to do with the plant after it has finished blooming. Do you cut the flower spikes or not? Will they produce more flowers?

Orchids such as *Oncidium*, most *Paphiopedilum, Cattleya, Vanda*, and *Cymbidium* only bloom once from a flower spike and will only flower again on newly produced spikes the following season. The spike that once held the flowers will wither and die. Once it turns brown, cut the flower spike with a clean tool and dispose of it. Dying flower spikes can attract insects, and removing them helps prevent the spread of certain pests and diseases.

For many *Phalaenopsis* and some *Phragmipedium* orchids, however, the stems can continue to bloom for longer periods. Many phragmipediums bloom successively over many months, producing more flowers and buds as the stem grows longer. Some varieties will even rebloom the following year on the same stem. For these slipper orchids, don't cut the stem until it dries up.

After a *Phalaenopsis* has flowered, it can continue to bloom from smaller secondary flower spikes that grow from the nodes, the joints along the flower stem, and can produce additional buds that extend the blooming season for weeks. Cutting the stem just above the third or fourth node from the base of the plant can encourage it to make more flowers. This is only recommended for strong plants with healthy leaves and root systems. If continually forced to bloom, some orchids can actually flower themselves to death. Some growers would rather the plant conserve its strength, since most often these secondary flower spikes are smaller and produce fewer flowers.

After the flowers have fallen off, you can remove the primary flower spike even if it's healthy and green. This doesn't harm the plant, and in fact helps it to begin recovering from the exhaustive flowering process. To remove the spike, use a sterile tool and cut it about 1 inch above the point where it connects to the plant. By extending the time a plant has to grow between flowerings, the orchid is able to produce more and larger blooms the next season.

Phragmipediums can continually produce blooms and buds for more than a year from the same inflorescence.

TERRA COTTA POTS

Terra cotta (unglazed clay) pots are a popular option for growing many plants, as they are inexpensive and decorative and have a classic appearance. They have a good weight, which can help counterbalance some top-heavy plants and prevent them from toppling over. When choosing pots, it's best to select those with thin walls to take advantage of the porous nature of terra cotta.

Unlike plastic, the porous surface of terra cotta allows moisture to be wicked away from the root system, which helps the plants dry out and adds to the drainage capability. Some terra cotta containers are designed as specialized orchid pots and have additional cuts or holes in the sides. These orchid pots allow for more air circulation and drainage at the roots, but as a result can also require more watering. Clay pots are relatively heavy and can prevent tall or top-heavy plants from tipping over. However, when a large number of pots are grouped together, the weight can become considerable on a windowsill, shelf, or bench. Many orchids will happily attach themselves to terra cotta pots, making repotting a challenge and requiring the pot to be broken to free vigorously rooted plants. Since terra cotta pots are porous, they can accumulate salts from water and fertilizers over time, which can make the pots unsightly and even problematic for some plants. When reusing terra cotta pots, it is recommended that you soak them in a 10% solution of bleach and scrub off any roots or soil that is stuck to their surface to prevent diseases from spreading in an orchid collection.

CERAMIC POTS

Glazed ceramic pots are a popular option when orchids are displayed for sale. However, most of these types of containers are more decorative than they are functional for growing plants for the long term.

Unfortunately, many of these pots do not have drainage holes in them and can hold water, which causes the base of the orchid to remain excessively wet or even submerged at times. If the container does have drainage holes, the glazed surface will hold in moisture, unlike a terra cotta pot, and the plants will dry slowly between watering. Although decorative ceramic containers can be used to cover, disguise, and provide weight to other pots, always ensure that the container has sufficient drainage and that the plants do not sit in water for any length of time.

ORCHID BASKETS

Wooden orchid baskets are an attractive and sometimes necessary choice for growing certain types of orchids. These slatted wooden baskets made of cedar or teak can be great for growing plants outdoors, where they can be watered freely.

Orchids with rambling growth habits or others such as *Vanda* that like to have their roots exposed do well in these wooden baskets, often filling them with roots and growth quickly. The baskets provide open air flow and rapid drainage for the plants—similar to growing attached to a mount or branch in nature. As plants outgrow smaller baskets or need repotting, the basket can simply be placed into a larger one without disturbing the root system. While quite nice to look at, however, growing plants in slat baskets can be a challenge in the home because the baskets dry out rapidly, requiring higher than average humidity and frequent watering to supply the growing plant with moisture. If the spaces between the wood slats are small enough, fir bark or moss can be added to hold moisture around the roots and provide more substrate for root growth.

POTTING MIXES

Orchids are adaptable and durable plants that can survive in seemingly unhospitable conditions in the wild. When cultivated under artificial conditions, as long as their basic needs are met orchids can grow and thrive in almost any potting mix.

Orchids appreciate good air movement around their roots. Some varieties, like this *Leptotes bicolor*, perform best when planted in open baskets and provided with ample water.

Over the years, growers have experimented with a variety of different mediums from wine corks to stone products to materials made from recycled tires, all with varying degrees of success. Natural materials such as osmunda fiber and tree fern, which are both derived from the stems of ferns, were once commonplace as orchid growing mediums, but due to concerns of overharvesting and unsustainable practices for the long term, their supply in the market has diminished greatly. While experimenting with different growing mediums has resulted in vast improvements for growing orchids commercially and in our homes, the basic components have stayed tried and true for many years. Every couple of years a new medium comes along and is touted as the "next big thing," yet most orchid growers still have the best success with bark or sphagnum moss mixes.

The variety of mixes available can also depend on your geographic region, with some materials being locally abundant in one area of the country and rare in another. Rather than produce an exhaustive review of the complete range of materials suitable for orchid mixes, which could be a list upward of forty materials, we will instead focus on fir bark, charcoal, sponge rock, sphagnum moss, and coconut fiber/chunks, which are commonly available and have proven over time to grow a diverse range of plants well.

FIR BARK

Perhaps the most widely used material for home orchid growing is the bark of conifer trees, including Douglas fir and Monterey pine trees harvested for paper or wood. Rather than see these materials wasted, they have been utilized by several industries including horticulture. Fir bark is a popular medium not just because orchids like to grow in it but it has many qualities that make it a near ideal medium for the plants. It is naturally decay resistant, breaks down slowly over time, and allows free drainage and air circulation around the roots of plants. Fir bark can also hold some moisture without becoming oversaturated, thus avoiding a soggy root system. It also mimics the rough-textured surface of tree bark that orchid roots are naturally adapted to attach to, providing a similar environment for the root system to grow on and around.

Fir bark is available in several different sizes to suit the roots of various orchids. Fine bark (¼-inch diameter), also called seedling bark, is suitable for fine-rooted, terrestrial, or miniature orchid varieties such as *Paphiopedilum* and *Miltoniopsis*. Medium bark (½-inch diameter) has more coarse texture in a container and is suitable for a large range of plants including *Phalaenopsis, Cattleya, Oncidium*, and many *Dendrobium* orchids. Coarse or large bark (1-inch diameter) is generally suitable for thick-rooted plants and those that prefer good air circulation around their roots, such as *Vanda* and some larger *Cattleya* orchids.

CHARCOAL

Horticultural charcoal derived from hardwood is commonly added to mixes to help maintain drainage. As bark mixes begin to break down over time, the charcoal helps to maintain pore spaces that allow water to continue to drain and keep the roots healthy and growing. Charcoal's chemical properties allow it to buffer a mix and prevent it from becoming too acidic due to natural acids in the bark or acids produced from fertilizers applied to the plants. Over time, it will help keep the pH balance of the potting medium more even and prevent acidification of the mix, which can be problematic for some orchids.

Like fir bark, horticultural charcoal is available in different sizes that match with the diameters of the fir bark used in a variety of orchid potting mixes.

SPONGE ROCK

Perlite is a porous, crushed volcanic glass and soil mix additive that is familiar to many gardeners. Sponge rock is also volcanic, and its larger particle size (¼- to ½-inch diameter) makes it an ideal additive to orchid mixes. Orchid roots need a proper balance of moisture and air around the roots, and the addition of a small percentage of sponge rock helps with drainage and the integrity of the mix over time to prevent the loss of the air spaces needed for healthy root systems. Sponge rock is also chemically inert, meaning that it will not alter the chemistry of a potting mix but only aid in ensuring the mix retains its ability to freely drain water.

SPHAGNUM MOSS

Sphagnum is a living moss found in bogs around the world but largely harvested from temperate regions, with most of the material used for orchid culture originating in Chile and New Zealand. The long strands of the moss are harvested, dried, and then packed for use in growing and propagating plants. Sphagnum moss is widely used, especially for the production of *Phalaenopsis* for the mass market. It has proven to be a nearly ideal medium for some kinds of orchids because it's relatively sterile, slightly acidic, and highly absorptive, holding many times its dry weight in moisture. Even though the medium is saturated, the water is held within the dry cells of the moss, allowing the orchid access to moisture but also providing the necessary air spaces around the roots.

As a growing medium, sphagnum moss presents some challenges because it behaves much differently than bark in a container. Plants grown in sphagnum need to be evenly moist—not overly saturated or too dry—a difficult balance to maintain in some growing conditions. If sphagnum moss is allowed to dry out, it can be difficult to remoisten properly, so it should not be allowed to go bone dry between watering.

COCONUT FIBER/CHUNKS

Concerns about sustainability and renewable resources have encouraged orchid growers to explore alternatives to fir bark and other commonly used materials. The use of coconut husk products—both in chunks similar to fir bark or ground into a fibrous material—has found favor among orchid growers, especially in tropical areas where the supply is more abundant. Coconut fiber is becoming more of a staple material in orchid growing as the quality and supply have increased and orchid growers have found that some plants, such as dendrobiums and cattleyas, perform well in it. Coconut products hold more moisture than an equivalent volume of bark because they are composed of densely packed natural fibers. Due to this water-holding capacity, some growers are using it as an additive to their orchid bark mixtures to prolong the periods between watering.

BASIC ORCHID MIX RECIPES

Recipes for orchid potting mixes are as diverse as those for the perfect apple pie or martini. While everyone agrees that the end result is a healthy orchid that blooms and survives well, how the mixes are created can lead to some debate. Orchid growers must learn over time how a certain combination of ingredients behaves in their particular conditions and make adjustments based on their watering habits, container choice, and types of plants that they like to grow.

Some basic mixes work well for many types of orchids, and they are best measured in proportions so you can mix as much or as little as you need depending on whether you're potting one plant or a hundred. The materials are available from orchid nurseries and suppliers, although nowadays even your local nursery may carry orchid potting supplies. Many orchid supply companies have pre-made mixes tailored for specific groups of orchids. If in doubt, check with another local orchid grower or nursery about which mixes work best for which plants in your particular region. With observation on how quickly the containers dry between watering, the two recipes presented here can be modified to suit your conditions, containers, and watering habits.

When mixing or working with dust-producing ingredients such as charcoal, perlite, or even bark, it is recommended that you rinse the materials first, work in a well-ventilated area, and wear a mask to prevent breathing in the dust, which can be irritating.

Terrestrial Orchid Mix

This basic mix is suitable for orchids such as *Paphiopedilum* and *Phragmipedium*, as well as fine-rooted plants like *Miltoniopsis*, smaller *Cattleya*, and *Oncidium*.

2 parts medium fir bark
1 part fine fir bark
1 part sponge rock
1 part charcoal

Epiphytic Orchid Mix

This basic mix is suitable for *Cattleya*, larger *Oncidium*, *Dendrobium*, *Phalaenopsis*, *Cymbidium*, and *Vanda*. (For *Vanda* orchids grown in containers, substitute large bark for medium bark.)

3 parts medium fir bark
1 part sponge rock
1 part charcoal

PROPAGATING
from a Keiki

Occasionally some orchids produce plantlets from the pseudobulbs or flower spikes. Each plantlet is a smaller identical clone of the parent, called a keiki (pronounced KAY-kee), the Hawaiian word meaning "baby" or "child." The production of keikis can be encouraged with the use of specialized propagation hormones applied to the nodes of the flower stem, which causes the dormant bud to develop into a plant rather than a flower stem. Many *Phalaenopsis* orchids naturally produce keikis on the older flower stems if they're not cut from the parent plant after blooming. The production of keikis is also common in *Dendrobium* orchids, which produce them along the pseudobulbs as the plants get older and larger. If exposed to the wrong cultural or environmental conditions for flowering, such as warm night temperatures or not providing a dry rest period, many types of dendrobium will make keikis rather than flowers.

Propagating a plant from a keiki is not difficult, but it requires some patience and the proper timing. The plantlet must be large enough to survive on its own without the food and water provided by the parent. As a keiki begins to develop, it produces stems and leaves before making any roots. Once two or three roots have developed, it can be carefully removed from the parent stem with a sharp blade, cutting just where the plantlet joins the stem. Some growers wrap the base of the fresh-cut keiki with a small pad of moistened sphagnum moss to help retain moisture and provide protection for the new roots as they develop. Pot up the plantlet as you would for any other orchid, and make sure that it gets a little extra water and care while the root system develops. Once the small plant has established itself, you can water and fertilize it like you do the parent plant.

Keikis provide a way to propagate a plant identical to the parent. After they produce roots, keikis can be potted up and grown to blooming size.

REPOTTING AND DIVIDING ORCHIDS

One of the most nerve-wracking experiences for a novice orchid grower is repotting these precious plants. Many growers hesitate out of fear and caution. By waiting too long, however, the plant is put in greater jeopardy of having problems than if it was repotted sooner. Knowing the right time to repot an orchid is based on the time of the year and some observation of the growing plant. You'll eventually develop a routine for the plants in your collection to keep them thriving for many years to come.

In an ideal situation plants should be repotted every 2 to 3 years, before the growing medium starts to break down. When this happens, the open spaces in the mix needed for the proper balance of moisture and air around the orchid's roots start to disappear, which can eventually suffocate the plant and cause the roots to rot. Decomposing bark often gathers at the bottom of the pot in a saturated layer that looks like coffee grounds, impeding drainage and keeping the plant oversaturated between watering.

For many orchids, there is a preferred time of the year to repot based on their growing season. The best time to repot is relatively soon after flowering as the plant begins producing new roots and leaves for the following growing season. Once the plant has initiated visible new roots with green growing tips, it is a good time to consider giving the plant a fresh mix. The growing root tips are delicate and can

New roots are produced at the base of new growth. They are easily identified by their bright green growing tips and white coloring. Take care not to damage the growing root tips when handling or repotting the plant.

be damaged easily during repotting; they should be less than 1 inch long to avoid snapping them off during the repotting process. If you are not sure when the ideal time to repot a plant is or no new growth is evident, you can wait about 2 to 3 weeks after flowering to repot. Don't repot while a plant is producing flower spikes, buds, or blooming. Such disturbance to the root system can cause the buds to drop off and not develop or shorten the lifespan of the blooms if they are already open.

The process of repotting an orchid is relatively simple. Depending on the growth habit of the plant—whether monopodial or sympodial— the technique that gives the best results varies slightly. The plants will appreciate their new home and reward you with new roots, leaves, and flowers.

REPOTTING A MONOPODIAL ORCHID

Phalaenopsis and *Vanda* are examples of monopodial orchids, which grow from a single stem upward. The plants produce leaves sequentially one above the other along the single stem, growing upward and taller with age and sometimes producing roots along the stem as well as at the base of the plant. When monopodial orchids have grown for a long time, the roots may creep over the edge of the pot and the lower leaves may drop off, exposing the stem and eventually making the plant look leggy.

Materials

pot or container

newspaper

potting mix

pruners or straight razor blades

pencil

plant labels

1 Choose a container for the plant based on the existing root system, one that is only slightly larger than the mass of roots. It is best to have the roots snug and filling the entire volume of the container. If reusing a container, clean and sterilize it by soaking it for several hours in a 10% bleach solution and scrubbing off any dirt or old roots, which will help prevent the transfer of pests and diseases between plants.

2 Place a layer of newspaper on your work surface to make cleanup easier. (If repotting more than one orchid, removing a few sheets of newspaper between plants is an easy way to provide a clean surface to prevent any diseases from being transferred.)

3 Remove any labels or plant tags and place them in a small container so they don't get lost during the repotting process.

4 Prune away the old flower spikes from the plant.

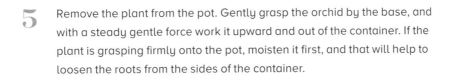

5   Remove the plant from the pot. Gently grasp the orchid by the base, and with a steady gentle force work it upward and out of the container. If the plant is grasping firmly onto the pot, moisten it first, and that will help to loosen the roots from the sides of the container.

6   Remove the old potting medium by gently working it away from the root system. Gently shake the medium off and use your fingers to loosen the pieces of bark, then work the root system open while being careful not to damage it.

7   Use the pruners or razor blade to groom the plant by removing any dead or dying roots or dead leaves. Healthy roots are silver green or tan, whereas dead roots are usually dark brown and blackened. However, the color of the roots does not always indicate their health, as some roots might become stained by the bark over time. If in doubt, see if they are firm by gently squeezing them with your fingers. Healthy roots are firm to the touch and not soft and hollow. Don't forget to clean and sterilize your tools between plants to avoid spreading pests or diseases. Cleaning tools with alcohol or bleach will only guard against some pathogens, and only heat sterilization will kill orchid viruses on tools. Using a disposable razor blade to cut plants is an easy way to prevent the spread of viruses.

8   Roll up a couple of sheets of newspaper around the old bark and dispose of it, as bark that is broken down is not suitable for reusing.

9   Place the groomed plant on the newspaper and ready the container by placing a small amount of potting medium in the bottom. (Adding crock or other materials is not necessary, as you don't want to impede the water flow or drainage out of the container in any way.)

10   Gently place the roots into the pot. Turning the pot as you insert the plant can help to wind longer roots around the inside of the container. If the roots are stiff and difficult to maneuver, moisten them under the sink with tepid water to make them more supple and flexible.

11

13

15

11 Position in the plant in the center of the container with the roots extending outward from that point. The lowest leaf should be even with the edge of the container. While holding it with one hand, start adding potting medium around the roots.

12 Add handfuls of potting medium around the roots, gently working the bark down among the roots of the plant. Tapping the pot on the work surface helps to settle the bark in the container. Continue adding potting mix until the container is full and there are no large spaces between the roots and the potting mix. There should be about ¼ to ½ inch of space from the top of the potting medium to the base of the lowest leaf.

13 Gently press down on the potting medium at the edge of the container and continue all around the circumference of the pot. This helps to firm up the potting medium and make good contact between the roots and the potting mix. Be careful, though, because pressing too hard around the base of the plant or the surface of the potting mix can actually damage and crush the roots below.

14 Once the plant is firmly in place, water it well with tepid water, while allowing the water to flow freely through the pot. This flushes out any small particles created during repotting, saturates the potting mix, and allows you to ensure that water is able to flow easily down through the pot and out the bottom.

15 Add a plastic label with the name of the plant and the month and year it was repotted. Replace old or broken labels, as they will become brittle and unreadable over time. Using a pencil is best, because it will not fade. Return the plant to the growing area, and water and fertilize it as normal.

REPOTTING A SYMPODIAL ORCHID

Cattleya, Dendrobium, and *Oncidium* are examples of sympodial orchids, which produce pseudobulbs in a tight clump or across the surface of the potting medium from a horizontal thickened stem called a rhizome. The roots are produced along the rhizome and at the base of the pseudobulbs. Occasionally a rhizome will fork, and the plant will begin to grow in more than one direction. If a sympodial orchid is allowed to grow for too long in the same container, it will look like it's trying to escape by creeping out over the edge in different directions, with the roots hanging in the air or gripping the outside of the pot. Repotting this type of orchid requires a slightly different technique to accommodate the lateral growth habit of the rhizome.

A rhizome clip is used to secure the newly repotted plant, helping it to take root.

Materials

pot or container

newspaper

potting mix

pruners or straight razor blades

rhizome clip

pencil

plant labels

1 Choose a container for the plant based on the existing root system, making sure that the roots will fill the entire volume of the container without excess space. The container should have enough space to allow for 1 to 2 years of growth for the horizontal rhizome. Use a new container for the best health of the plant.

2 Place a layer of newspaper on your work surface to make cleanup easier. (If repotting more than one orchid, removing a few sheets of newspaper between plants is an easy way to provide a clean surface to prevent any diseases from being transferred.)

3 Remove any labels or plant tags and place them in a small container so they don't get lost during the repotting process.

4 Gently grasp the plant by the base and with a steady gentle force work it upward and out of the container. If the plant is grasping the pot firmly, moisten it first to help loosen the roots from the sides. If that doesn't work, you might have to break the old pot to make it easier to remove the plant, especially if the roots are attached to the outer surface of the container.

5 Remove the old potting medium by gently working it away from the root system. Gently shake the medium off and use your fingers to loosen the pieces of bark, then work the root system open while being careful not to damage it.

6 Use the pruners or razor blade to remove any dead or dying roots, old flower stems, or dead leaves. Healthy roots are silver green or tan, whereas dead roots are usually dark brown and blackened. Healthy roots should feel firm to the touch and not soft and hollow. Some of the oldest pseudobulbs might be shriveled or have little or no roots or leaves attached to them. If this is the case, remove the older pseudobulbs by cutting through the thickened rhizome just behind the last healthy pseudobulb. Keep at least three or four healthy bulbs, as divisions smaller than that are difficult to keep growing.

7 Roll up a couple of sheets of newspaper around the old bark and dispose of it, as bark that is broken down is not suitable for reusing.

8 Place the plant on the clean newspaper surface. Ready the container by placing a small amount of potting medium in the bottom. (Crock or other materials are not necessary, as you do not want to impede the drainage in the container.)

9 To position the orchid, place the end of the creeping rhizome toward the edge of the pot with the newest growth pointed toward the center of the pot. There should be enough distance from the newest growth to the edge of the pot for 1 to 2 years of growth before the plant would be over the edge of the new container.

10 Place the roots into the pot by gently turning the pot and winding them around the inside.

11 The rhizome should be just below the edge of the pot, about ½ to 1 inch from the rim of the container. While holding the plant in place, gently work potting medium around the roots. Tapping the pot on the work surface helps to settle the bark in the container. Continue adding potting mix until the container is full and there are no large gaps between the roots and the potting mix.

12

15

12 Once the container is full, the rhizome should be just at or slightly below the growing medium no deeper than ½ inch. Gently press down on the potting medium at the edge of the container, continuing all around the circumference of the pot and firming up the potting medium. Don't press hard along the rhizome to avoid damaging the roots or possibly separating the roots from the rhizome.

13 Use a rhizome clip to secure the plant in the pot and hold the plant in place. (If the plant is too unstable it will not root well, and additional stakes can be used to help support the plant until it's firmly rooted in the pot.)

14 Once the plant is firmly in the pot, water it well with tepid water while allowing the water to flow freely through the pot. This flushes out any small particles created during repotting and saturates the potting mix. Make sure that water is able to flow easily down through the pot and drain out the bottom.

15 Add a plastic label with the name of the plant and the month and year it was repotted. Replace old or broken labels, as they will become brittle and unreadable over time. Pencil is best, as it will not fade. Return the plant to the growing area, and water and fertilize it as normal

GROWING ORCHIDS ON A MOUNT

The majority of tropical orchids are epiphytes, and growing them on a mount not only provides them with similar conditions as found in the rainforest but re-creates the look of life in the trees. It also highlights the plants' miraculous ability to thrive and bloom without any soil while clinging to a branch.

Epiphytic orchids such as *Tolumnia*, some *Cattleya*, and many miniature orchids prefer growing on a mount because they require air about their roots at all times and grow poorly when placed in pots. Other plants, including many miniature orchids, adapt well to growing as mounted specimens, making them easier to manage and water outside of small containers.

Growing orchids on a mount can be more of a challenge than in a container because mounted plants require more exacting control of the environment for them to grow and bloom properly, especially in the home. Mounted plants require more frequent watering and a higher average humidity. For some species, nearly daily misting or watering is necessary to prevent the plants from becoming dehydrated. Also, with little or no medium to conserve water and fertilizer for long periods, mounted orchids require regular applications of food to provide them with nutrients for proper growth and flowering

Materials

piece of cedar or manzanita or a cork slab

rigid wire (a coat hanger works well)

wire snips

needle-nose pliers

electric drill

sphagnum moss

fishing line

1   Choose a suitable mount for the plant that will allow for a few years of growth. Durable wood such as manzanita or cedar work well, or orchid suppliers can provide cork or tree-fern slabs. Not all woods are suitable for orchids, but untreated cedar is amenable. If you are using a piece of drift-wood, soak it in clean fresh water for 24 to 48 hours to make sure any salts have been leached out.

2   Select a healthy epiphytic orchid with a vigorous root system and one that is producing new roots and growth. Take the orchid out of the pot and gently remove any of the potting medium from the roots.

3   Moisten the sphagnum moss and squeeze out the excess water, leaving the sphagnum damp to the touch.

4   Loop a length of fishing line around the mount to tie on the sphagnum moss. Place a small pad of moistened sphagnum moss no thicker than ¼ inch deep onto the mount to give some moisture to the roots of the plant. Crisscross with the fishing line to secure.

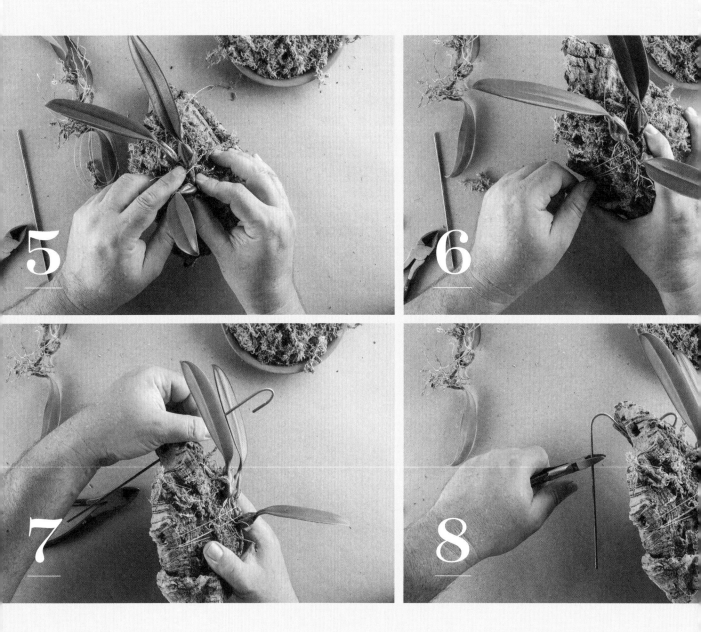

5   Fan the plant's roots over the surface of the mount, and lightly cover them with an additional thin layer of moistened sphagnum. Make sure new growth is positioned parallel to the slab when possible so the new roots can quickly attach themselves to the mount.

6   Using another length of fishing line, wrap the roots and moss snugly but not too tightly to prevent the fishing line from cutting into the roots. Make several passes across and around the mount in different directions to secure the roots and moss in place. (Until the plant attaches itself to the mount, you might need temporary additional support for the plant's growth to keep it upright.)

7   Cut a piece of the rigid wire and punch it through the mount. You might have to use a drill to make a hole for the wire, if the mount is hardwood or especially thick.

8   Use the pliers to form the wire into a hook, so the mount can be hung in its final location. Clip off any excess wire.

9   Water or mist the mounted plant and place it in bright indirect light until you observe new root growth. Once root growth has begun, the plant can be moved to a brighter location if necessary. Be sure to water and fertilize regularly, while allowing the plant to dry slightly between watering.

DIAGNOSING PLANT PROBLEMS

To grow orchids successfully in the home, you need to know how to water and feed your plants, but you also need some basic knowledge of how to tackle any problems the plants might encounter. Inspecting your plants on a regular basis is important for spotting minor problems and correcting them before they become major ones. The chart on pages 73–74 will help you diagnose common orchid problems and make the necessary corrections to get your plants back on the right track for their best growth and blooming.

COMMON PESTS AND DISEASES

Prevention is one of the best forms of pest control. Maintaining a clean growing area free of weeds and dead plant material, providing the proper environment, and keeping your plants healthy will prevent pest, bacteria, fungi, and virus populations from growing unnoticed. Keep watch on your plants to make sure that you spot the signs of pest infestations and infections early and eliminate them quickly. Some pests, such as scale, mealybugs, and mites, require three or four applications of pesticides or other treatments to eliminate the adult insects and the eggs that can hatch over time, so routine and repeat applications are advised to keep them under control. However, pest infestations do not always have to mean the use of harsh chemical pesticides. Small populations can be controlled through softer approaches such as using a strong jet of water to dislodge bugs, treating with soapy water, applying horticultural oils, or even introducing beneficial insects such as ladybugs. Many bacterial, fungal, and viral diseases can be controlled or even eliminated by modifying or correcting cultural practices or the growing environment, for example, by increasing air circulation or ensuring that plants remain dry after dark.

REHABILITATING A SICK PLANT

Despite our best efforts, sometimes the health of a prized orchid can go in a negative direction quickly. There are a few things you can do to help the plant rehabilitate and recover from damage or pests and start producing new leaves and roots and eventually blooming again. The process will take some time and extra effort, but the reward is worth it, especially if the plant is special or has some sentimental value.

If the sick plant is flowering, the first thing to do is remove any flower spikes or blooms. Flowering requires a large expenditure of energy from the plant. As difficult as this might be, removing any existing blooms is the fastest way to conserve the plant's energy and stimulate it to begin growing again.

If the plant has a healthy root system, you are already off to a good start. If not, repotting the plant is probably necessary. Root disease and failure of the root

PLANT PROBLEMS

Problem	Cause	Remedy
Dark brown or black spots on leaves	bacteria or fungal infection	Bacterial or fungal infections on leaves are often caused by water sitting too long on the foliage. Make sure the infection is not spreading, and treat with a fungicide or appropriate pesticide if necessary. Increase air circulation and/or water in the morning, and allow the plant to dry before nightfall.
Brown leaf tips	too much fertilizer or irregular watering	Brown leaf tips often result from excess fertilizer or a buildup of salts in the potting medium. Cut back on fertilizer or repot to remove excess nutrients. Make sure plants do not get too dry between watering.
Sticky droplets on leaves	insect infestation	Some plants produce sticky droplets naturally on flower spikes, and it's nothing to worry about. If there are clear sticky patches on leaves, it could be signs of an insect infestation. Inspect the plant closely for pests. Rinse with soapy water or treat with an insecticide.
Leaves and bulbs shriveled	dehydration or poor roots	Increase watering or humidity to help prevent the plant from dehydrating. If the plant is receiving sufficient water and it is still shriveled, the roots have probably rotted or died and are no longer able to absorb water. Repot and inspect roots for signs of damage or disease.
White or light brown patches on leaves	sunburn or temperature burn	Move plant to a more shaded location out of direct sunlight. This type of damage can occur rapidly, especially if the conditions have changed or the plant was moved to a different location.
Young leaves turning brown	bacterial rot	Water sitting in the new growth or crown can often lead to soft brown rots that will cause the new leaves to die. Water plants early in the day to allow them to dry by nightfall, and try to keep water out of new growth.
Leaves yellowing and falling off	bacterial infection, age, or overwatering	Plants naturally drop older leaves toward the base or on older pseudobulbs, especially after flowering and as new growth is produced. If newer leaves or many leaves are falling off, increase air circulation and treat with a fungicide or appropriate pesticide.
Weak elongated stems and leaves	lack of sunlight	Increase sunlight to the plant gradually, if possible, to avoid burning the foliage.
Silver or brown streaking on leaves and/or flowers	thrip or spider mite infection	Pests such as thrips and mites can be hard to see with the naked eye. Inspect leaves with a magnifying glass, and treat with an appropriate pesticide if they are found.

Problem	Cause	Remedy
Dark brown or black watery spots on leaves	bacterial rot	Water sitting on foliage for long periods can encourage bacterial and fungal rots, especially in warm weather. Water plants and allow their leaves to dry by increasing air circulation. Treat with fungicide if rot is substantial, and remove any diseased or damaged foliage to prevent infections from spreading.
Large holes in leaves and/or flowers	slugs, snails, or chewing insects	Chewing pests can destroy flowers quickly. Snails and slugs leave visible shiny trails on stems and flowers, and grasshoppers and roaches can chew flowers up as well. Inspect plants at night; search in hiding places under pots and drainage holes to eliminate the pests.
White cotton-like substance on leaves and/or flowers	mealybug infection	Mealybugs are sucking insect pests that often hide in masses of cottony growth on the backs of flowers and in the crevices of leaves and stems. Dislodge with a jet of water and treat with an appropriate pesticide.
Flower buds dropped before opening	stress to plant while flowers developed	A sudden change in the environment (temperature, humidity, and even air pollution) can cause flower buds to yellow and fall off. Providing too much or too little water will also cause a similar response. Keep plants away from drafts or extremes in temperature, and provide proper watering while buds are developing.
Plant not blooming	improper food, temperature, or light	Excess fertilizer can create luxuriant growth with no blooms. Reduce the amount of fertilizer or change to a fertilizer with lower nitrogen to encourage flowering. If plants do not receive a proper temperature regime, including a drop in night temperature, flowering will not be initiated. A lack of light will also prevent a plant from blooming. Gradually increase light levels or supplement with artificial lights.
Flowers contorted and not opening	lack of humidity or improper watering	If plants are allowed to get excessively dry at the roots or humidity is too low, flowers will not open properly. Increase watering and humidity around the plant.
Flowers with brown spots	water on blooms	Water left on flowers after dark will result in fungal spotting. The damage will be mostly cosmetic but can spread if the humidity is too high. Increase air circulation and keep water and misting away from the flowers.
Roots brown and not growing	overwatering	If a plant has been overwatered, it is best to repot, trim dead and dying roots, and place the plant in fresh mix.

COMMON PESTS AND DISEASES

Pest/Disease	Symptoms	Remedy
Mealybugs	cottony white clusters or insects often hidden on the plant among flowers and leaves	Use a jet of water to dislodge insects and treat with soapy water or insecticide repeatedly to eliminate. Groom plants by removing hiding places like dry sheaths and old leaf bases.
Thrips	silver or dry edges on flowers and damage to roots, flowers contorted and unable to open properly	Difficult to control; best treated with repeat applications of an insecticide. Regular syringing of leaves and flowers with water can help reduce populations.
Scale insects	yellow spotting on leaves, with brown or white shell-shaped insects attached to the surface of leaves and stems	Remove old sheaths and other hiding places. Treat with insecticide or soapy water to kill adults. Use a soft cloth or jet of water to dislodge insects to help eliminate the adults and their eggs.
Aphids	green or brown sucking insects clustered on tender new growth or flowers and buds	Spray with a jet of water to remove the insects and treat with soapy water, horticultural oils, or insecticide to control.
Spider mites	very small crawling arachnids, silver and brown streaking or pitting of foliage occasionally with webbing	Use proper pesticide to control or treat with soapy water or horticultural oils. Introducing beneficial predatory mites and syringing foliage with water can help control populations.
Slugs and snails	slime trails and chewed new growth and flowers	Inspect plants and check under pots, especially after dark. Keep watch for slime trails and remove.
Bacterial and fungal diseases	brown or black soft spots and patches on foliage, often with an odor	Modify cultural practices and increase air circulation. Use fungicides or appropriate pesticides only if infections are widespread and damaging.
Viruses	brown or black streaking on leaves and flowers, especially noticeable on new growth, and disfigured blooms	Remove infected plants and dispose of them, because viral infections cannot be cured. The best control is prevention: using clean and sterile tools and preventing insects that carry viruses, such as thrips and aphids, from spreading.

system—especially from overwatering—is one of the most common causes of death in orchids. If this is the case, when you remove the plant from the pot, the roots will be brown, soft, and often foul-smelling, indicating that the roots were oversaturated and died. Remove any potting medium and dead roots like you would for regular repotting of a healthy plant. In many cases the leaves and bulbs will be shriveled and dehydrated, which is another sign that the roots have been compromised and no longer can provide enough water for the plant. Once the plant has been groomed to remove any dead tissue, allow it to air-dry. Some growers dust the plant with ground cinnamon, the same as in your kitchen, to help dry the roots and serve as a natural fungicide.

To rehabilitate the root system of a sick plant, one of the best potting mediums is sphagnum moss. The moss is naturally acidic, which prevents the growth of bacteria and fungi, and can help hold the right balance of moisture and air to stimulate new roots. Wrap the roots in the sphagnum moss and plant in a snug container. Place it in a shaded location to prevent the plant from becoming dehydrated in bright light and higher temperatures. Increasing the humidity around the plant will help it considerably. If you do not have an area in your home that has higher humidity, you can place the plant in a loose open plastic bag or open-mouthed container out of direct sunlight to act like a mini greenhouse, which will help it recover from the loss of roots. Water the plant sparingly and keep the humidity up. Wait until the plant has started to form a few new roots before you start regular watering and feeding again.

GROWING ORCHIDS IN THE OPEN GARDEN

Growing orchids doesn't have to be a strictly indoor hobby. Many types can be grown outdoors in the open garden in both temperate and tropical areas. Like indoor growing, evaluating the available light, water, and temperature conditions will help you to determine which plants might do well in your outdoor garden. Understanding summer and winter high and low temperatures and talking to experienced orchid growers in your local area will also help you to choose plants that will not only survive but thrive in the garden. An easy way to incorporate orchids into the landscape is to place indoor plants outdoors for the summer, bringing a bit of tropical flair to the home garden.

GROWING OUTDOORS IN TEMPERATE CLIMATES

Although their tropical cousins always seem to steal the spotlight, there are many hardy orchids that grow well in temperate gardens. Orchids like the hardy lady's slippers are among the short list of Holy Grail plants for the woodland gardener. When positioned correctly in the garden, these orchids can thrive for many years among hostas, ferns, and other familiar perennials. Their reputation as being difficult to please has made hardy orchids prized rarities, but horticulturists are beginning to master the propagation and cultivation techniques needed to make these plants more widely available from specialty perennial nurseries. Choosing the right hardy orchid for your garden requires a little bit of research to get the right plant for the right place.

Cultivating tropical orchids outdoors in the summer can be easy, as many of the techniques for watering, fertilizing, and potting of plants in the home can be applied. Outdoor growing conditions will be more variable when it comes to temperature, humidity, and watering needs because of the plants are exposed to the elements.

Hardy lady's slippers (*Cypripedium*) have long been prized by gardeners who were able to acquire and grow these rarities. Doing well in a shady acid woodland alongside other shade perennials, they are among the most beautiful of spring-blooming perennials. Soils with abundant humus and well-drained structure suit them best. Their brightly colored slipper flowers borne on delicate stems above pleated foliage make them a

Cypripedium kentuckiense is a hardy lady's slipper that thrives in shady woodland gardens.

crown jewel of a woodland garden. Lady's slippers grow well in dappled sunlight in well-drained soils. They require a little extra attention but are worth every bit of effort. Advances in their culture and hybridization by a group of dedicated North American and European horticulturists has made these iconic woodland wildflowers available in the commercial market around the world. Many of the newly created hybrids are easier and more vigorous than their wild counterparts and make excellent subjects for the open garden.

One of the most vigorous and forgiving of all garden orchids is the Chinese hyacinth orchid (*Bletilla striata*). It is not only easy to grow, but can be cultivated in a wide range of garden conditions and geographic regions. The flowers are borne in shades of pink and white, but the most common color form has deep magenta pink flowers that resemble miniature *Cattleya* blooms. Other forms with variegated foliage have been selected for added interest. *Bletilla* orchids are less particular about soil conditions than other terrestrial orchids, and any well-drained garden soil with some shade and moisture suits the clumping plants, which can spread over time to make quite a display. Their long strap-like leaves add to the textural interest in the garden when the plants are out of bloom.

An often underappreciated group of hardy orchids is the genus *Spiranthes*, named for the spirally arranged flowers that are delightful additions to the garden. One of the most vigorous is *Spiranthes odorata* 'Chadds Ford', which blooms in late summer to early fall with 12-inch-tall spikes of diminutive sweetly fragrant white flowers. It spreads slowly in moist sandy acidic soils and even grows well in wet boggy conditions where many other plants don't thrive. If conditions are right, it will self-sow in the garden, popping up in other areas and producing small spreading colonies over time.

The European terrestrial orchid flora has some spectacular species that are now starting to gain in popularity for American gardens. The genus *Dactylorhiza* has long been popular in English gardens. These orchids are appreciated for their brightly colored magenta purple to pale pink flowers. The plants often have foliage that is spotted and patterned with dark purple, adding to their garden interest. The clumps produce many tall (up to 24 inches) flowering stems in May to June and make attractive and exotic-looking garden specimens. The plants prefer cool, moist, acidic soils similar to the wet meadows or marshes

Many orchids will thrive in outdoor gardens if you have the right climate and temperatures year-round for the plants.

they occur in naturally, and they adapt to garden conditions well if their moisture needs are met. *Dactylorhiza* orchids prefer cooler temperatures around their roots; in areas with hot humid summers, planting in part shade is best to keep the plants happy and growing for years to come.

Japan is home to several terrestrial orchid species that are suited for North American gardens. The genus *Calanthe* has been extensively hybridized and cultivated in Japan for many years. Despite their beauty and popularity in Japanese horticulture, however, they are still relatively unknown in American gardens. *Calanthe* orchids are excellent subjects for the woodland garden, growing best in an open, well-drained, woodland soil with good amounts of organic matter. They perform well in milder winter areas (USDA Zones 7–9) and can add a tropical look with their broad evergreen pleated foliage topped in spring with spikes of colorful flowers in shades of red, pink, yellow, green, and bronze, often with a contrasting colored lip.

GROWING OUTDOORS IN TROPICAL CLIMATES

Several areas of the country including southern California, parts of the Pacific Northwest, and much of southern Florida provide excellent conditions for growing some types of orchids in the open garden. Like all other garden plants, the high and low temperatures throughout the year determine the types of orchids that will succeed in your climate. In central California, for instance, *Cymbidium*, some *Dendrobium*, and species orchids such as *Laelia anceps* thrive in the sunny days and occasionally cold nights, whereas warm-growing orchids such as *Phalaenopsis* and *Vanda* would suffer during periods of cold or cooler weather. In southern Florida where freezes are uncommon, warm-growing plants such as *Cattleya, Vanda*, and *Phalaenopsis* can be grown outdoors year-round with little or no difficulty.

In tropical climates, orchid plants can be un-potted and attached to the branches and trunks of trees, allowing them to grow epiphytically as they would in the wild. The plants are best placed as new root growth begins, which allows them to root quickly onto the surface of the bark. Attach the orchids with sisal twine, cotton string, or any other natural material that will break down over time once the plant has established itself and has a firm grip on the tree. Newly planted orchids might require some additional water until they are well established. Outdoor growers also place their plants in open-sided shade or lath houses to provide some protection from sunlight and weather while allowing the orchids to grow in the open air.

Growing orchids outdoors is not necessarily easier because you have less control over temperature, water, and sunlight than if the plants were grown indoors. Many outdoor growers have to face extremes in weather, battling hurricanes and rainstorms that can damage collections in a short time. Aside from extremes, constant monitoring of the weather is necessary to make sure that plants are protected from damaging temperatures, as even in these warmer areas temperatures near freezing or below can occur from time to time. In the event of an approaching cold front, keep the plants drier at the roots and move them indoors under shelter; if they have to remain outdoors, cover them with a bed sheet or other thin cloth to help insulate and protect the foliage from frost damage. You also need to be vigilant about making sure orchids grown outdoors receive enough water, and supplement with irrigation when needed.

Once established in the garden, many orchids will survive with little or relatively no care and grow for decades, producing spectacular blooming specimens in the landscape. To learn which orchids grow best outdoors in your area, consult with local nurseries or other orchid growers nearby and learn from their successes. Growing tropical orchids outdoors in the right climate is a sure way to complete the look of a tropical garden paradise. If you run out of space on the ground, adapt like orchids have and start gardening in the trees.

Pl. CCCCCI

ANOECTOCHILUS LOWI hort.

ANŒCTOCHILE DE LOW

Orchidées

Les Anœctochiles sont de charmantes Orchidées terrestres, dont les feuilles étalent, sur un champ velouté d'un vert obscur, des réseaux d'or ou d'argent à brillants reflets métalliques. Tout l'art du peintre échoue à rendre, dans leur suave fraicheur, les nuances de cette riche broderie dont la nature s'est plue à les orner.

L'*Anœctochilus Lowi* est à la fois une des plus belles et des plus rares d'entre ces plantes à coquettes parures. Son nom spécifique dit assez qu'on doit son introduction à la maison Low de Londres.

Ainsi que nous le disions dans notre précédente Chronique, les Anœctochiles reviennent à la mode et font leur réapparition dans les collections. Elles n'avaient d'ailleurs été délaissées que parce qu'elles étaient devenues anémiques, incultivables, à force d'avoir été torturées et soumises à des traitements de culture impossibles.

Aujourd'hui que de nouvelles importations sont venues donner aux jardiniers des plantes saines, pleines de vigueur, nous leur conseillons de les cultiver simplement, *sans tour de force*, comme ils cultivent les autres Orchidées.

Mais voilà la difficulté ; l'Anœctochilus est si extraordinaire qu'il n'y avait qu'une culture extraordinaire qui pût leur réussir ! Il fallait une chaleur énorme au pied, et sous ce prétexte, on leur préparait un lit spécial, ayant une quarantaine de degrés de chaleur minima, la plante était encore recouverte

Seasonal Care CALENDAR

- Carefully watch spikes, leaves, and stems near windows, as freezing temperatures can create cold drafts that may freeze leaves and flowers if they are placed too close to windows.

- Heaters in our homes help to keep us and our plants warm, but they also reduce humidity. Monitor the moisture in the air to prevent damage to plants and certain pests, such as spider mites. Add humidity trays or even a humidifier to help orchids get through the dry months of winter.

- The colder gray days of winter slow the growth of many plants. Cut back slightly on fertilizer, both in frequency and concentration, to ensure you don't overfeed slowly growing plants, which can force weaker growth that can be more susceptible to pests and diseases.

- Watering with cold water or leaving water on the foliage can cause damage and water spotting on plants, especially with warm-growing varieties.

- Placing plants on heaters or above them can overheat and dehydrate them quickly. The high temperatures desiccate the plants and can encourage certain pests and diseases.

- Watch for emerging flower spikes, and moderate any wide swings in temperature and humidity by providing a consistent environment for the developing flower buds. This will prevent the plant from being shocked, which causes flower buds to yellow and drop off prematurely.

ODONTOGLO... CORONARIUM

Vanda Cathcarty LINDL.
Himal. Sikkim (Serre chaude)

- As the days grow longer and light intensities get stronger, watch for yellowing leaves and possible burning of plants, especially lower light varieties such as *Phalaenopsis* and *Paphiopedilum* orchids.

- Watch for developing flower spikes on spring bloomers like many *Phalaenopsis, Cymbidium, Miltoniopsis,* and some *Oncidium,* and be careful not to break them when handling or watering plants.

- Stake developing flower stems early so the flowers can grow and display their best.

- With longer days and an increase in temperatures, the danger of insect pests such as aphids increases. Be vigilant and watch to make sure they don't get out of control.

- Some orchids begin vigorous growth spurts in spring. Repot as necessary to make sure plants have fresh potting mix and plenty of room to grow. Be sure to have pots and potting mix on hand so you can be ready to repot plants at the right time.

- Start increasing fertilizer to ensure that growing plants have plenty of nutrients for the developing growth and flowers.

- Spring can mean wide and rapid fluctuations in temperature and humidity in some areas. Monitor your growing area to prevent unexpected problems from changing temperatures.

SPRING

- Remove old flower spikes on spring-blooming orchids to encourage the plants to start growing.

- As plants are actively producing new leaves, shoots, and roots, make sure they are repotted correctly and fertilized regularly to get the best growth for next season's blooms.

- Move plants outdoors when temperatures are consistently above 50°F at night and all danger of late frosts have passed. Place the plants in a shaded location to prevent them from burning with the sudden change in light intensity going from indoors to out.

- Watch for flowers developing on summer-blooming orchids such as *Vanda* and *Oncidium,* and make sure they are staked to support the blooms.

- The heat of summer can be rough on some cooler growing orchids, such as *Masdevallia* or *Miltoniopsis.* Make sure that they get plenty of water and air movement to keep them cool.

- Although air conditioning can be comforting for us during hot weather, for many orchids the rapid drop in humidity and cool temperatures can cause problems. Make sure plants have plenty of water and the humidity remains high.

- Intense summer sunlight can burn plants, even indoors. Keep plants out of strong direct sunlight, protected from midday sun, and behind a sheer curtain to prevent damage to the leaves.

- Increasing air circulation helps to reduce leaf temperatures and cuts back on the chance of burning or fungal and bacterial diseases.

- Many warm-growing plants will be putting on their strongest growth, so make sure they get plenty of water and fertilizer.

- Warm weather also means more insect, slug and snail, and other pest activity. The higher humidity can also mean fungal and bacterial diseases will be on the rise. Keep a close eye on the plants for early signs of pests and disease.

- In periods of high temperatures, be careful when treating plants with pesticides. Don't apply pesticides if temperatures are above 85°F, especially horticultural oils.

- Avoid repotting cooler growing varieties, such as *Masdevallia* or *Miltoniopsis,* as the additional stress of repotting during hot weather can really set them back.

- Prepare the indoor growing area before plants have to be moved in. Clean out humidity trays, growing shelves, and other surfaces and replace bulbs in light fixtures for a clean start for the indoor growing season.

- If your plants are kept outdoors in the summer, keep an eye on night temperatures to make sure they don't get damaged by sudden or unexpected frosts.

- As temperatures drop, plants such as *Cymbidium,* nobile dendrobiums, *Cattleya,* and many *Paphiopedilum* orchids initiate flower spikes. Take advantage of natural drops in temperatures to help harden off growth and encourage flowers in the following months.

- Ensure plants are dry before nightfall, as the cooler days will cause the plants to dry off more slowly and can invite fungal and bacterial diseases.

- Start to reduce fertilizer to prevent rapid growth. Now that light levels are decreasing and days are getting shorter, the growth of many plants slows.

- Monitor plants and pots for slugs, snails, and other pests to prevent bringing unwanted guests indoors with your orchids.

- Make sure that all but the most cold tolerant plants are indoors before the temperature drops below 55°F. All it takes is one unexpectedly cold night to damage plants beyond recovery.

- The foliage on *Catasetum* and nobile dendrobiums begin to turn yellow and drop as the plants enter dormancy for the winter. Start to withhold water to guarantee flower buds and prevent the plants from rotting.

- Keep night temperatures cool for *Cymbidium* orchids and cool-growing *Dendrobium* to make sure that the flower spikes continue to develop. A rapid rise in temperature can cause the flower spikes to stop growing.

- If you have not repotted plants, it's better to wait until late winter to spring. Plants will appreciate less disturbance when root and shoot growth has slowed.

introduction à la maison Low de Londres.

Ainsi que nous le disions dans notre précédente Chronique, les Anœctochiles reviennent à la mode et font leur réapparition dans les collections. Elles n'avaient d'ailleurs été délaissées que parce qu'elles étaient devenues anémiques, incultivables, à force d'avoir été torturées et soumises à des traitements de culture impossibles.

Aujourd'hui que de nouvelles importations sont venues donner aux jardiniers des plantes saines, pleines de vigueur, nous leur conseillons de les cultiver simplement, *sans tour de force*, comme ils cultivent les autres Orchidées.

Mais voilà la difficulté ; l'Anœctochilus est si extraordinaire qu'il n'y avait qu'une culture extraordinaire qui pût leur réussir ! Il fallait une chaleur énorme au pied, et sous ce prétexte, on leur préparait un lit spécial, ayant une quarantaine de degrés de chaleur minima, la plante était encore recouverte

CYPRIPEDIUM SUPERBIENS

from *Select Orchidaceous Plants* (1865–1875) by Robert Warner

THE NEW YORK BOTANICAL GARDEN

JEWEL ORCHID TERRARIUM

93

DECORATIVE ORCHID TERRARIUM

97

ORCHID PENJING

121

WOODLAND GARDEN ORCHID CENTERPIECE

127

ORCHID PROJECTS

ORCHID WREATH **103**

ORCHID KOKEDAMA **109**

ORCHID BONSAI TREE **115**

MINIATURE ORCHID MOBILE **133**

ORCHID SCULPTURE **139**

HANGING ORCHID GALLERY **145**

JEWEL ORCHID TERRARIUM

Jewel orchids are one of the few groups of orchids that thrive in the humid environment of a terrarium over the long term. Often found in shaded humid locations in the forest understory, they are perfectly adapted to this kind of cultivation. Dozens of orchid species that have exquisitely patterned and variegated leaves are called jewel orchids. The leaves are best showcased where they can be viewed closely, revealing networks of sparkling metallic veins and intricate patterns laid across velvet foliage. Jewel orchids mix and match easily, creating endless combinations that are a visual and horticultural feast for the eyes.

Materials

terrarium or glass-walled container

charcoal or gravel

sphagnum moss or soilless mix

decorative sheet moss

large tweezers or chopsticks

decorative stones

spray bottle

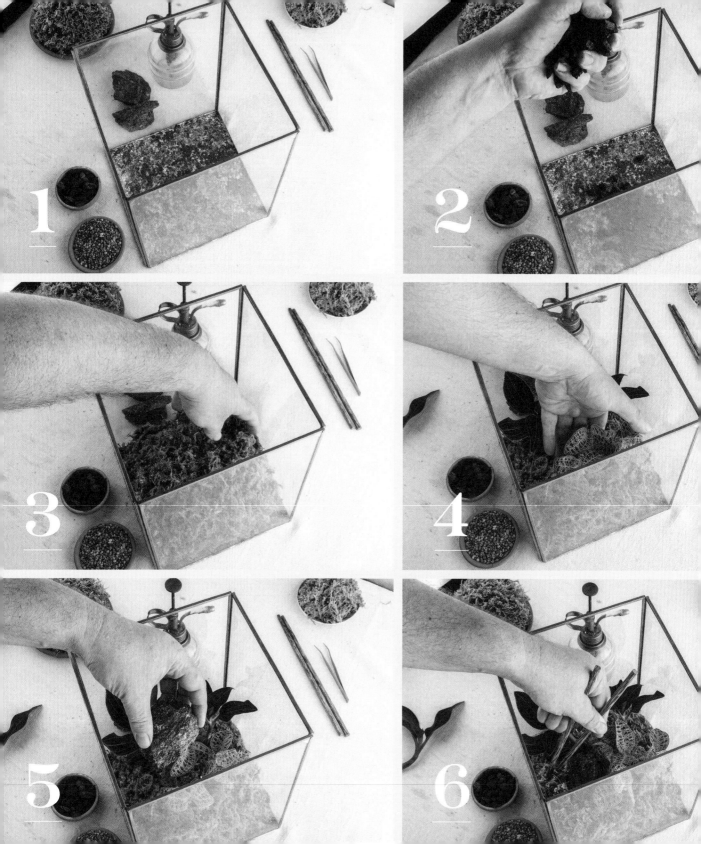

1. Choose a glass-walled container that is watertight and provides enough space for the plants and for you to easily work in. Decorative glass containers, fishbowls, or even wide mouth jars work well for this type of planting. Clean the container and prep it for the planting project to begin.

2. Place a ½- to 1-inch layer of washed gravel or charcoal on the base of the container. This layer allows water to drain, so the roots and planting medium do not get too saturated.

3. Jewel orchids grow well in sphagnum moss or a peat-based soilless mix (ProMix) with added perlite for drainage. Moisten the planting medium slightly before placing it in the terrarium and it will be much easier and less dusty to work with. If you use a soilless mix, place a 1-inch layer at the bottom of the container.

4. Arrange the plants in the terrarium according to your liking, making sure that the roots are buried in the substrate. Using the tweezers or chopstick can help you maneuver soil and moss around the base of the plants in a tight space.

5. Add decorative stones, driftwood pieces, or other companion plants to add visual interest to the terrarium and to help create the look of a miniature landscape.

6. Place a layer of decorative sheet moss over the top of the planting substrate to give a finished look. Mist the foliage and sheet moss with the spray bottle and use it to wash down the interior of the glass.

Project Care

Jewel orchids prefer lower light conditions and grow best out of strong direct sunlight. Place the finished terrarium in bright but not direct sunlight, otherwise the terrarium can easily over heat and harm the plants inside. Water and fertilize the plants on a regular basis, and groom any dead or dying foliage out of the terrarium when it appears. Keeping the terrarium groomed helps to prevent any fungal or other diseases from occurring in the humid environment.

DECORATIVE ORCHID TERRARIUM

One of the best and most attractive ways to overcome low humidity in the home environment is to place orchids in terrariums with other plants. All plants release moisture into the surrounding air, and grouping them together with some mosses creates a localized area of higher humidity that will benefit all the plants, not just the orchids, and helps flowers last longer. Leaving the top of the container open allows for air circulation and prevents the still conditions that would shorten the life of the blooms or even the plant itself. Orchids well-suited to life in a terrarium include *Masdevallia, Paphiopedilum,* and many miniature orchids. Setting up a terrarium of this type is simple, and the choice of your container can reflect your personal style and décor.

Materials

terrarium or glass-walled container

charcoal

gravel

sphagnum moss

companion plants

decorative sheet moss

large tweezers or chopsticks

decorative stone or wood pieces

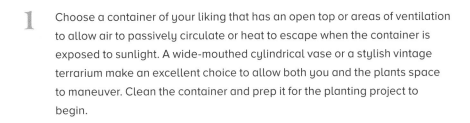

1 Choose a container of your liking that has an open top or areas of ventilation to allow air to passively circulate or heat to escape when the container is exposed to sunlight. A wide-mouthed cylindrical vase or a stylish vintage terrarium make an excellent choice to allow both you and the plants space to maneuver. Clean the container and prep it for the planting project to begin.

Select companion plants that will do well for the light levels and conditions for your orchid and final display location. Plants such as ferns, *Peperomia*, *Philodendron*, *Pilea*, and *Fittonia* are easy-care plants that thrive in terrarium conditions.

Arrange the plants together to get an idea of how the final design will look and to test the size of the plants in height and width against the size of the container that you wish to use. This helps to ensure that all plants have room to grow without overcrowding. It will also save time, trouble, and damage from rearranging the plants in your design.

Prepare your materials by moistening the sphagnum moss and decorative sheet moss with warm water to make it easier to work with and reduce any dust it might produce.

2 Place a 1- to 1 ½-inch layer of rinsed horticultural charcoal or gravel on the bottom of the terrarium to provide drainage and prevent the plants' roots from sitting in water.

3 Use a shallow layer of substrate—either coir or sphagnum moss—to plant into. This layer allows plants to root and grow and wick up extra water, preventing an oversaturated root zone in the terrarium.

4 Lightly mound up and pack the moss around the roots of your foliage plants, leaving room for the orchids.

Decorative Orchid Terrarium

5 If you disturb the roots of many orchids while they are in bloom it will shorten the flowers' lifespan, so the orchids should be left in their original pots and placed into the terrarium. Empty plastic pots of similar sizes can be used as place holders while you shape and maneuver your foliage plants into their final locations. Leaving the empty pots in place allows you to easily exchange plants as one finishes blooming and another can be moved into the terrarium as it comes into bloom. Place the orchids into the terrarium and arrange so the flowers and foliage are not overcrowded and have some space around them.

6 Once you have all of the plants in place, reposition any plants that look too crowded or need to be straightened. Be careful as you work within the terrarium so you don't damage any of the buds or blooms of the orchids.

7 Place a layer of moistened decorative sheet moss as the top dressing to give a finished look and hide any containers or sphagnum moss that is showing. Use large tweezers or chopsticks to position moss in tight spaces to avoid damaging the plants. The addition of some decorative stones or pieces of driftwood can complete the vignette and give the terrarium more visual interest for display in your living space.

Project Care

Remember to keep terrariums out of bright direct sunlight, as they can easily heat up and dry out quickly. Mist regularly and check to ensure that all the plants are receiving the proper amount of water.

ORCHID WREATH

Combining blooming orchids with other epiphytic and succulent plants in a wreath is an elegant way to incorporate living plants into a decoration for anytime of the year. The orchids can be kept in their containers for easy watering and removed on occasion or replaced when they are done blooming. Mixing the textures of tillandsias and other bromeliads, succulents, and other natural decorative elements can make an unforgettable statement in the home or outdoors in climates that allow the plants to survive.

Materials

grapevine wreath

florist wire

needle-nose pliers

wire snips

Spanish moss

decorative sheet moss

tillandsias

Phalaenopsis orchids

fishing line or twine

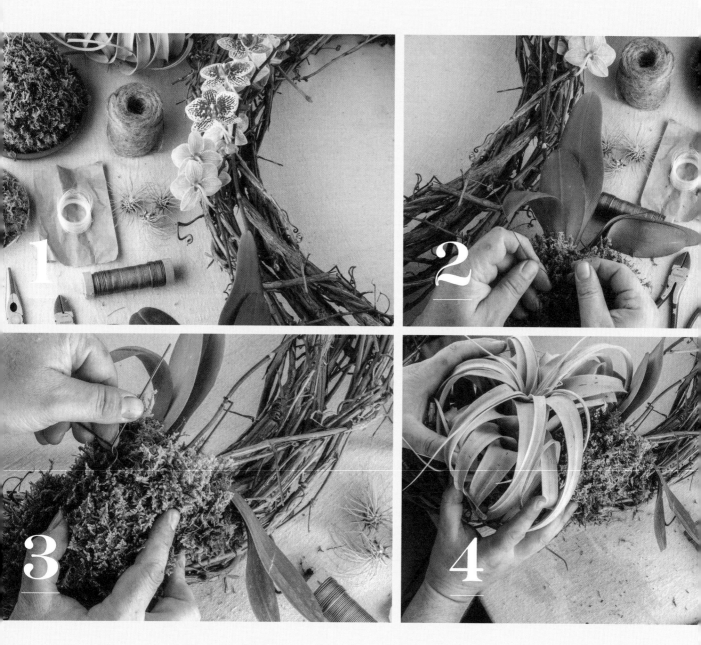

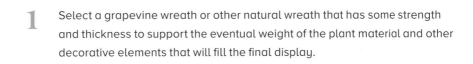

1 Select a grapevine wreath or other natural wreath that has some strength and thickness to support the eventual weight of the plant material and other decorative elements that will fill the final display.

* Using a heavy-gauge florist wire, make a loop or hanging hook around the wreath at the back to provide a location to hang the wreath in the location of your choice. It's not a bad idea to double up the wire for extra support.

* Some people find it easier to work with the wreath hanging when working on the placement and design, rather than on a flat surface, to get a better idea of how the wreath will look when it is completed.

* Start by tucking decorative moss or Spanish moss into the spaces between the grapevine to give a fuller and more naturalistic look.

2 Wrap the pots of orchids in moistened decorative sheet moss and hold it in place with fishing line or twine to camouflage the containers.

3 Start placing your plant material on the wreath with the largest plants first. Florist wire can be looped through the pots and then tied onto the wreath to hold the plants in place. Placing the plants slightly off center or at irregular intervals will look more natural and less manufactured.

4 Experiment with different placement patterns. Try heavier on top versus the bottom of the wreath or plants weighted toward the left or the right side of the wreath. The design and arrangement is entirely up to your taste. It can be as lush or as minimalist as you wish.

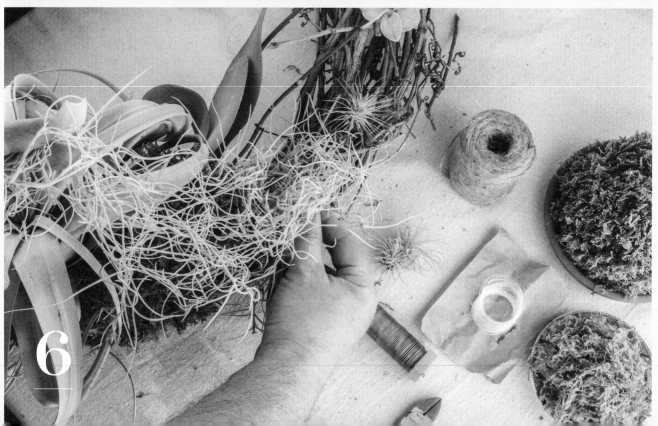

5   After the orchids are placed, start placing the smaller plants to fill in the space and your complete your design vision. Using other plants with their roots wrapped in moss such as ferns, bromeliads, or even succulents can give a striking compliment with varied textures and colors of foliage. Tillandsias are an excellent choice, as they do not require soil or moss to grow well and can be tucked into the grapevine or gently wired with florist wire into place. Other natural objects such as seedpods, pine cones, decorative fungi, bark, or even other types of wood or branches can be added to help give depth and textural interest to the wreath.

6   Once all the plants are in place, finish off the wreath with some more decorative moss or Spanish moss tucked among the orchids and other plants. This helps to conceal the florist wire, fills out spaces between the plants, and gives a cohesive look to the elements of the wreath. Stake any orchid flower spikes that need support and place the wreath in its final display location.

Project Care

Remember to mist and water the plants as necessary to keep your creation looking its best.

ORCHID KOKEDAMA

In kokedama, a traditional Japanese way of displaying plants, moss spheres can be used to create an acrobatic and visually stunning display in any space. Often referred to as a string garden, this sculptural way of growing plants is enjoying a surge in popularity due to interest in its minimalist aesthetic along with a steady presence on social media. The pot is removed from the equation, and the orchid is grown in a sphere of moss placed either in a shallow saucer or hanging in the air. Whether placed as a single specimen or a suspended grouping of kokedama, the visual impact of the floating floral spheres can be spellbinding.

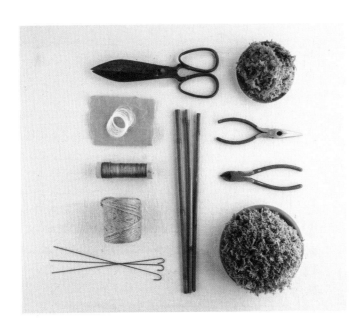

Materials

sphagnum moss

twine or fishing line

decorative sheet moss

needle-nose pliers

wire snips

florist wire

scissors

green plant stakes

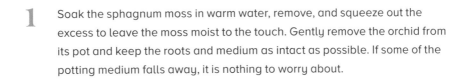

1   Soak the sphagnum moss in warm water, remove, and squeeze out the excess to leave the moss moist to the touch. Gently remove the orchid from its pot and keep the roots and medium as intact as possible. If some of the potting medium falls away, it is nothing to worry about.

2   Take a small handful of sphagnum moss and wrap it around the root ball of the orchid, building it slowly in all directions to form a sphere. It might take some practice at first to get the hang of it, but gentle pressure on the moss will help it stay in place as you continue. Build the sphere around the roots to a thickness of 1 to 2 inches around the original root ball.

3   Depending on your preference, choose either natural twine or less visible fishing line. Start winding the twine around the outside of the root ball. You do not have to pull the twine very tight but it should be snug enough to help hold and shape the ball of moss.

4   Continue crisscrossing the string until the sphere is supported and the root ball is snugly in place.

5   Tie off the string to hold it in place.

6   Take the pieces of decorative sheet moss and cut and trim with scissors where necessary. Wrap sheet moss on the outside of the sphagnum moss sphere until all sides are covered. If you are placing the kokedama on a platform or shallow decorative bowl, then you are done. If you wish to suspend the planting, continue with the next steps.

7

8

7 Using the needle-nose pliers, bend an open J-shaped hook in the one end of the wire. Carefully insert the straight end into the moss ball and press until it comes out of the top of the sphere near the base of the plant. The hook-shaped end will disappear into the base of the moss sphere and will help to provide support while the kokedama is suspended.

8 Using the pliers, bend the straight end at the top into a tight closed loop, which provides an attachment point for the hanger or string to suspend the completed kokedama.

- Test the plant in a hanging position, and stake any flower spikes or stems that need extra support to help balance the plant.

- Choose the final location for your plant or grouping and arrange hanging in place.

Project Care

Check the plants regularly for drying out, and water or soak the plants as needed.

ORCHID BONSAI TREE

Making an orchid bonsai tree gives a modern twist on an ancient horticultural art form. Instead of the painstaking work of miniaturizing a tree, you take that one step further by creating a miniature tree of orchids. A piece of driftwood is set into a bonsai pot, orchids are added to the branches to give the effect of a tree, and the orchids attach themselves, growing and blooming over time. You don't have to limit yourself to one type of orchid. Select a range of plant forms and blooming times to give changing interest throughout the year.

Materials

manzanita bonsai driftwood (available online) or other branch structure

sphagnum moss

bonsai pot

small stones

aquarium gravel

decorative sheet moss

fishing line

plastic-coated wire

needle-nose pliers

wire snips

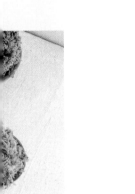

1   Start with a pre-constructed manzanita bonsai or select an interesting branch with good structure and form evoking a bonsai tree.

2   Choose an appropriately sized container, and arrange some sphagnum moss and decorative stones to act as a base for the tree.

3   Set the tree in place. You can also use plastic-coated wire to secure it the base of the pot. Moisten the remaining sphagnum moss and squeeze out the excess water, leaving the sphagnum damp to the touch.

4   Take a small portion of the moistened sphagnum and use the fishing line to tie it onto the upper side of a branch, gradually building up the moss until you get a small sphere. Continue until you have several branch sections covered. These areas will become the planting surfaces to which you'll attach the orchids. You can leave some branches exposed to simulate weathered or dead branches that would be found in nature.

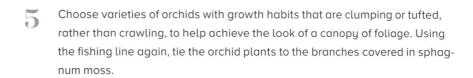

5 Choose varieties of orchids with growth habits that are clumping or tufted, rather than crawling, to help achieve the look of a canopy of foliage. Using the fishing line again, tie the orchid plants to the branches covered in sphagnum moss.

6 Continue until you have all the branches planted with orchids and, if you wish, companion plants such as tillandsias.

7 You can leave the surface of the container bare or give a more established look with a layer of decorative sheet moss.

Project Care

Mist and feed the plants regularly, and give the newly created orchid bonsai the right amount of light for the plants to establish and grow. Over time, the plants will require some grooming and care to shape their growth and the form of the bonsai tree.

Orchid Bonsai Tree

ORCHID PENJING

You don't need a lot of orchids to make a bold statement. The Chinese art of penjing uses decorative or sculptural rock along with miniature plants to create striking minimalist designs meant to evoke landscape scenes, with various plants creating the illusion of trees growing on distant mountains. Many orchids grow on sheer rock faces in nature, so they are perfectly adapted to this kind of culture and it mirrors the way they would be found in the wild. Penjing uses techniques similar to mounting an orchid on a piece of wood or cork, but using the surface or pockets in stone instead.

Materials

lava rock or decorative stones (available from bonsai suppliers or some specialty pet stores)

sphagnum moss

fishing line

decorative sheet moss

bonsai humidity tray or other shallow container

aquarium gravel or washed sand

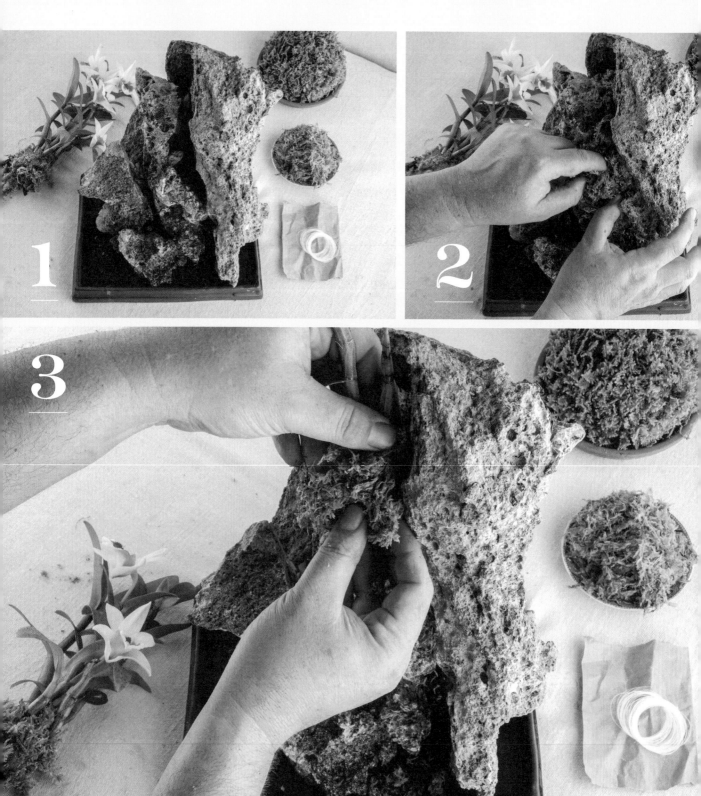

* Choose a suitable lava rock or use a grouping of stones affixed together with a waterproof adhesive. Lava rock can be drilled easily to create planting pockets for the orchids or other companion plants, such as small ferns, or other foliage.

1 Position the stone in the arrangement that you wish. Rotating the stone can expose interesting angles and show off the character of the stone, adding to the final visual interest. If the stone doesn't sit level on its own, it can be placed later in a bed of gravel or washed sand for stability.

* Moisten the sphagnum moss and squeeze out the excess water, leaving the sphagnum damp to the touch. Remove the orchid from its pot, and gently remove the potting medium.

2 Fill the intended planting pocket with loosely packed sphagnum moss to provide a substrate for the plant to root into and help secure it in place.

3 Insert the roots of the orchid into the pocket of sphagnum.

4   Top-dress with additional moistened sphagnum moss.

5   Using fishing line, tie the orchid in place. Make sure it is snug but not so tight as to cut into the roots.

6   Place a layer of decorative sheet moss over the surface. Use more fishing line to hold the moss in place over the roots to achieve a finished and established look for the plant.

•   Place the stone on the humidity dish or settle into decorative gravel or sand to support the stone in an upright position.

Project Care

Mist the surface of the moss regularly to keep the plant and moss growing well. If you wish, when the orchid has rooted to the surface of the stone and moss, the fishing line can be cut away and removed. Place the arrangement and humidity dish in a location where it will receive the proper amount of light for the orchid to grow and flower well. Water and feed the plant as you would for any other orchid in your collection, making sure to keep the dish filled with water to enhance the humidity.

WOODLAND GARDEN ORCHID CENTERPIECE

A rustic wooden container becomes the perfect foil for a grouping of *Paphiopedilum* orchids arranged with mosses, ferns, and other found or foraged objects. The arrangement captures the mood of the plants growing in nature and harmoniously blends a variety of natural elements to enhance the individual beauty of the foliage and flowers of the lady's slippers. It makes a striking focal point as a table centerpiece or a decorative way to display prized plants while they are in bloom.

Materials

decorative container

Paphiopedilum orchids and companion plants

seedpods, branches, pine cones

decorative sheet moss or moistened sphagnum, reindeer moss, and decorative fungi

florist wire

fishing line

heavy plastic sheet

needle-nose pliers and scissors

misting bottle or paintbrush

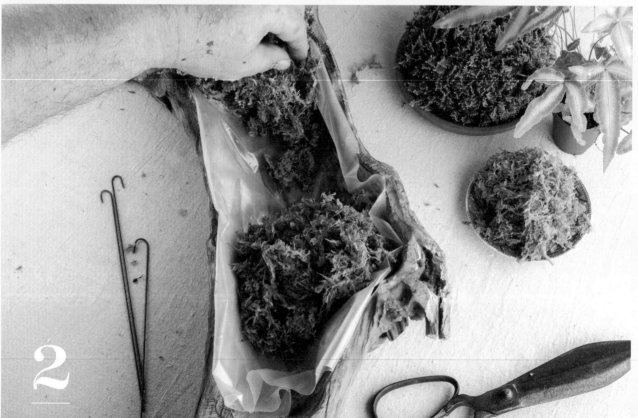

• Gather decorative materials such as interesting branches, foliage, stones, seedpods, or other natural elements from either a craft or florist supply or forage local seasonal materials if you're able to.

1 Prep the container by placing a plastic sheet to prevent water from leaking out.

2 Place a thin layer of decorative sheet moss or sphagnum into the container as a base to work on.

• Stake the flower stems to support the blooms and protect them while working. The orchids should be kept in their containers. Arrange the plants on the workspace surface in the design that you wish to create. This will allow you to move plants around and see how they look with different arrangements and heights before you start to put the container together.

3   Once you have a design you like, place the plants into the container and use decorative moss to help support and space them. Add other companion plants to fill out the space conceal the containers of the orchid plants.

4   Use scissors to trim and shape decorative sheet moss to conceal the root balls and pots of the plants in the arrangement. Continue adding decorative elements such as branches, seedpods, and pine cones to help fill out the spaces between the plants and give the illusion that the plants are growing in nature. To achieve a more natural look to the arrangement, be free and loose with your placement rather than tight and controlled.

•   Rotate the container and fill out any spaces making sure that there are no bare spots and it can be viewed from both sides.

5   Place decorative sheet moss and reindeer moss into the small spaces between the orchids and other decorative pieces for the final touches to the centerpiece.

•   Use a dry paintbrush to clean off the surface of the decorative moss, if needed, and use a misting bottle to moisten the surface of the moss.

Project Care

Set the arrangement in its final location out of bright direct sunlight. Check the plants once a week, and add water as needed. When the orchids are done blooming, they can be removed and others put into their place to enjoy.

MINIATURE ORCHID MOBILE

Many miniature orchids would be lost on a windowsill. In addition, because of their tiny size, these orchids can be less forgiving in an unfavorable environment. By creating a living mobile with hanging glass spheres, you can bring the miniature plants up to eye level, where the foliage and flowers can be appreciated at their best. The open-sided spheres help to hold moisture, maintain humidity, and prevent the small plants from drying out. A small pad of green moss or even other miniature plants that are not aggressive growers will only help the plants grow. Hanging the spheres on a piece of driftwood or similar structure visually connects the individual pieces into one spectacular element, creating a wonderful way to grow, display, and enjoy your plants.

Materials

glass spheres
fishing line or thin decorative wire
sphagnum moss
decorative sheet moss
horticultural charcoal
large tweezers or chopsticks

* Assemble your materials on a flat work surface. To help maneuver the glass bubble terrariums, set them in a bowl to keep them from rolling around while you work.

* Moisten the sphagnum moss and squeeze out the excess water, leaving the sphagnum damp to the touch.

1 Place a ½-inch layer of charcoal at the bottom of the sphere to help with drainage and provide a space for excess moisture.

2 Add a layer of moistened sphagnum moss as a pad to place the orchids and air plants on.

* Depending on the orchids that you are using, there are two different methods for planting in the glass spheres. If the plants are miniatures, growing in small pots or on mounts, you can simply nestle the plants into the moss without disturbing them. If you are adding larger plants or wish to remove them from their containers or mounts, wrap the roots gently in moistened sphagnum moss, tie the small moss ball together with some fishing line, and then add them to the glass spheres. Wrapping the roots in moss ensures good contact between the roots and moss, allowing them to access moisture for growth.

3
___

4
___

3 Place the orchids into the glass spheres, and arrange them to allow space for them to grow.

4 Using the tweezers or chopsticks, which make it easier to work in small spaces, add a layer of decorative sheet moss and other items for interest, such as tillandsias or driftwood pieces.

• Attach fishing line or thin decorative wire to the spheres, making sure the knots are tight and secure enough to support the final planted weight.

• Suspend the planted glass spheres in their final location from hooks anchored either into the ceiling or a branch to give an effect similar to a mobile. Vary the heights for interest and easy access to the spheres.

Project Care

Place the spheres in bright indirect light, and mist the plants heavily on a regular basis to provide moisture and humidity for them to grow.

ORCHID SCULPTURE

When mounted on a wall or hanging in a window or other well-lit space, a sculptural piece of driftwood can be transformed into a hanging garden with tillandsias and orchids. This is a perfect option for a small orchid collection where shelf or windowsill space is limited or nonexistent. In time, the orchids will attach themselves to the structure like they do in nature, creating a living sculpture that will grow and evolve and enhance any space.

Materials

driftwood

fishing line

picture frame wire

eye screws

wire snips

needle-nose pliers

florist wire

sphagnum moss

decorative sheet moss

tillandsias or other bromeliads

Spanish moss

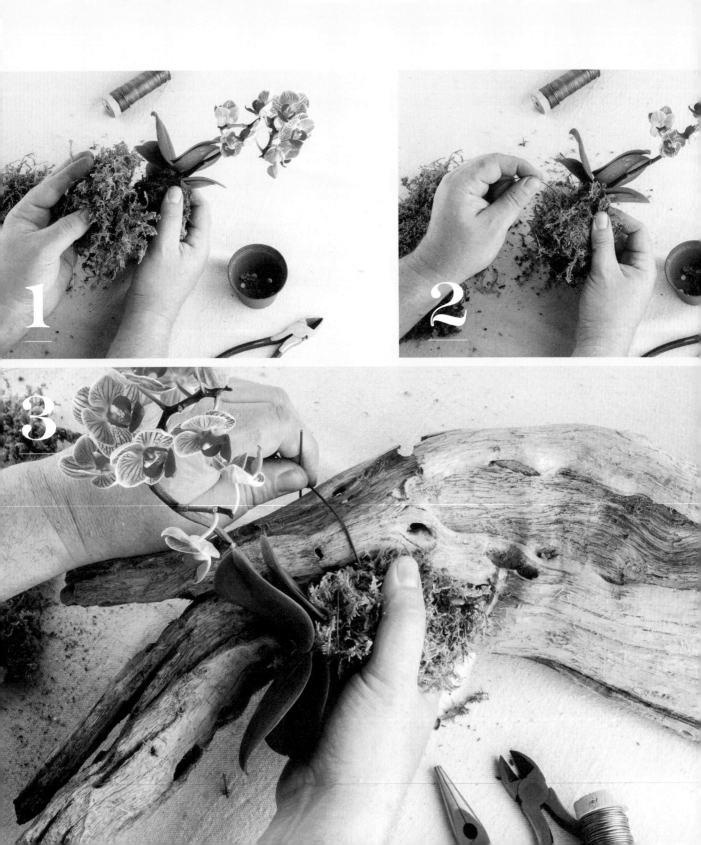

Choose a large piece of driftwood or join several together to create a framework to build a hanging garden upon. Driftwood is best purchased rather than harvested, because untreated driftwood may contain salts or even unwanted pests that could be brought into the home. Driftwood is often available in specialty pet supply stores or craft stores or from online sellers.

Choose the direction and orientation the driftwood piece will hang in, and place two eye screws at opposite ends of the wood. Attach picture frame wire to provide a sturdy hanger for the piece.

Moisten the sphagnum moss and squeeze out the excess water, leaving the sphagnum damp to the touch.

1 Unpot and prep the orchids and bromeliads. Wrap their roots in sphagnum moss and then decorative moss.

2 Secure the moss around the root system with fishing line.

3 Lay the orchid against the driftwood in the location that you wish it to be secured. Using a long piece of florist wire, secure the root ball against the driftwood and tie off at the back, making sure that the roots are secure and don't move easily. If the plant does move easily, repeat with another piece of florist wire.

Continue tying the orchids onto the driftwood. Step back from your creation occasionally to see if there are any adjustments that need to be made before continuing.

4

5

4 Place the bromeliads on the driftwood, filling in the spaces between the orchids and making sure that the driftwood sculpture remains balanced in weight when hanging.

5 After the last plants are secured in place, tuck in strands of Spanish moss around the base of the plants to add another dimension of interest.

Hang the driftwood planting in its final location. The types of orchids you choose in your sculpture will determine the proper growing location. Bright indirect light is best if you are unsure of where to place the sculpture, so plants get enough light to grow and bloom well. Avoid strong direct sunlight and drafty areas near doors and windows, if possible.

Project Care

Mist all plants on a frequent and regular basis to ensure they are getting adequate moisture. If they are drying out quickly, move the sculpture to the sink and give it a good shower to thoroughly saturate it. Groom and fertilize monthly and replace or reposition any plants that might have shifted. With proper care, the driftwood garden will grow and flourish for years to come.

HANGING ORCHID GALLERY

Whether you're drawn to the multitude of flower and plant forms offered or want an orchid collection but have limited space, miniature orchids can become addictive to collect. An excellent way to organize and display your collection is by grouping them in rustic decorative frames, giving the look of a green wall or vertical garden. Choosing a variety of plants with interesting growth habits and different bloom seasons can help create year-round interest. Tillandsias and ferns can be added for textural interest and to help offset and highlight the unusual flowers and forms of the orchids, and a backing of wire mesh with a pad of moss provides moisture to the roots. It is a creative way to take a cluttered jumble of plants and transform them into a horticultural masterpiece.

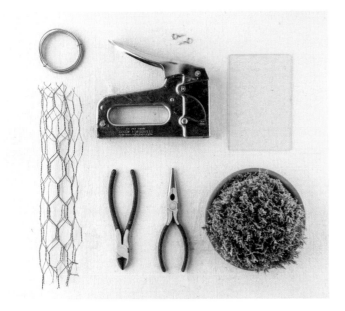

Materials

wooden picture frame

decorative sheet moss

1-inch wire poultry netting

Plexiglas or heavy plastic cut to size of the frame

screwdriver, small flathead screws, and eye screws

staple gun

wire snips

variety of miniature orchids mounted or in small pots

- Choose a picture frame that fits with your tastes and is durable and moisture proof. Rustic barn-wood frames look natural and are easier to work with than metal or plastic frames. Remove any glass or cardboard from the frame.

- Have a hardware store cut a piece of Plexiglas or plastic to the outside dimensions of the frame. Drill small holes at each corner for fasteners to hold it in place.

- Using the wire snips, cut a piece of poultry netting ¾ to 1 inch larger than the inside of the frame and place to the side.

- Moisten enough decorative sheet moss to fill the center of the frame.

1 Position the piece of cut poultry netting over the back of the frame and use the staple gun to secure it in place.

2 Lay the sheet moss, green side down, on top of the wire covering the opening of the frame.

- With gentle pressure, work the wire and moss into the opening of the frame, allowing the edges of the wire to flex, and flatten them down along the opening. Use additional staples to tack down the wire edges to hold them in place on the frame.

3

• Place the Plexiglas onto the back of the frame, and screw it into place. Be careful not to over tighten the screws and crack the Plexiglas. This plastic backing holds the moss in place and helps to keep moisture off the wall where you hang the completed frame.

• Turn the frame over and adjust or add any moss to areas where it is missing.

3 Arrange the miniature orchids on the face of the frame, hanging them from the poultry netting in an arrangement that is to your liking. Choose plants that have similar cultural conditions so they will grow well together. Add tillandsias or decorative moss to vary the texture and add interest.

Project Care

Hang the frame in the final location, making sure that the plants get the proper light and food they need to grow. Mist the plants and moss regularly to provide moisture, and give them a good soaking in the shower or sink on a regular basis.

Easy-Care ORCHIDS from A to Z

Aerangis luteoalba var. rhodosticta
Aergs.

Native to the cloud forests of central Africa, including Kenya and Cameroon, *Aerangis luteoalba* var. *rhodosticta* is one of the most beautiful of all miniature orchids. Small fans of foliage only a few inches in diameter—looking much like a miniature *Phalaenopsis*—produce wiry flower spikes shingled with cream to white blooms with a contrasting bright reddish orange central column. The long-lasting blooms are striking, and plants can produce multiple flower spikes from clumps of foliage over time. This variety is easily cultivated in intermediate to warm conditions. The small plants require even moisture and do well either mounted or in small pots. Do not allow them to dry out for too long during the growing season.

The delightful contrast of the bright orange column against the pristine white flowers makes *Aerangis luteoalba* var. *rhodosticta* a popular miniature species.

Angraecum sesquipedale
Ang.

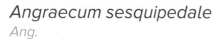

This species is one of the more famous in the orchid family because of its relationship with Charles Darwin and his theories on the moth that pollinates this Madagascar native. *Angraecum sesquipedale* bears magnificent large waxy night-fragrant blooms with a characteristic long nectar spur that dangles from the back of the flower, produced on a large *Vanda*-like plant with coarse roots. The plants grow well in warm conditions with even moisture and a well-drained potting medium. One caveat of this species is that it responds poorly to root disturbance during repotting. Any repotting should be performed carefully and with as little disturbance to the roots as possible, or the plant may take a considerable amount of time to recover and resume growing and flowering.

The fascinating biology and stately white fragrant flowers of *Angraecum sesquipedale* make it one of the most prized of all orchids.

Brassanthe Maikai 'Mayumi'
Bc.

A cross between *Brassavola nodosa* and the Central American *Guarianthe bowringiana* created one of the most vigorous and floriferous hybrids available. *Brassanthe* Maikai 'Mayumi' grows in multiple directions, but even smaller plants cover themselves with large flushes of bright pink flowers peppered with darker spotting, especially when grown in higher light conditions. The flowers inherited the sweet fragrance from the *Brassavola* parent and the late summer to fall blooming habit from *Guarianthe*. It is a superb plant for either the beginner or advanced grower looking for a compact plant that makes impressive specimens in short time. Even though this hybrid will flourish in a very wide range of conditions, plants grow and flower best when cultivated in bright light.

Brassanthe Maikai is a floriferous and colorful orchid that makes an excellent choice for beginning orchid growers.

Brassavola Little Stars
B.

A successful combination of two similar species has created a fantastic and floriferous result. This hybrid between *Brassavola cordata* and *Brassavola nodosa* is very popular with orchidists for the easy to grow plants that become large specimens covered with blooms in short time. The clusters of fragrant blooms are borne just above the long narrow leaves, and well-grown specimens are covered with light green and white blooms. *Brassavola* Little Stars does well in bright conditions with good drainage and is often grown mounted or in baskets to allow the roots to drain freely. This hybrid tolerates dry conditions and is a very durable and hardy choice for the beginning orchid grower.

The fragrant masses of blooms on *Brassavola* Little Stars make it a perennial favorite.

Brassavola nodosa
B.

Commonly called the queen of the night orchid, this wide-ranging species is found from Mexico through the Caribbean and into South America. *Brassavola nodosa* has long been popular with hobbyists for the durable and floriferous plants with white and green flowers that are tremendously fragrant in the evening. It is often suggested as an excellent beginner's plant. This species does well in drier conditions with bright light and a well-drained medium. The vigorous plants grow quickly and can cover a mount or a basket in short time, producing prolific displays of flowers in spring. When grown in the right environment, the plants can flower more than once a year.

The flowers of *Brassavola nodosa* produce their powerful sweet fragrance in the evening.

Brassia Rex
Brs.

Members of the genus *Brassia* are often called spider orchids, and rightfully so, with their enormous blooms that look like giant arachnids. The long filamentous sepals and petals of *Brassia* Rex can reach nearly 12 inches from top to bottom and never fail to attract attention. The flowers with numerous green and brown spots and bars create a beautiful symmetry and look more like a chorus line of dancers than creepy crawly critters. *Brassia* orchids enjoy bright light and good amounts of food and water when they are actively growing. When the plants are happy, they reward you with multiple spikes of flowers.

The large spidery blooms of a *Brassia* Rex in full flower look like they are dancing in air.

Bulbophyllum Elizabeth Ann 'Buckleberry'
Bulb.

This hybrid is one of the most bizarre and dramatic on this list of easy-to-grow orchids. A specimen with several flower spikes in bloom is an unforgettable sight. In late fall to early winter, the plant produces long wiry inflorescences, with a cluster of eight to ten pink speckled and striped flowers with long tails nearly a foot in length. The overall effect is otherworldly, with some comparing the blooms to jellyfish or other fantastic creatures. *Bulbophyllum* Elizabeth Ann 'Buckleberry' is a creeping plant that can make large specimens in a short period, doing best planted in a basket or shallow wide pot to accommodate the plant's growth habit. The plant requires even moisture throughout the year and warm somewhat shaded conditions to thrive.

Despite the blooms appearing exotic and unusual, *Bulbophyllum* Elizabeth Ann 'Buckleberry' is easy to grow.

Catasetum

Once only considered a genus of orchids for the serious collector, this group of orchids has experienced a surge in interest during the past few years. Using several closely related genera, hybridizers have created a group of colorful and pattered new hybrids that are increasing interest in these unusual orchids. The breeding has included recent breakthroughs in color including a range of plants with flowers that are so dark that they approach black and are considered to be the darkest orchid flowers on the market today. Many of the plants are deciduous and need a seasonal rest period. This requires a little more effort and observation to succeed, but the reward of the unusual and fragrant blooms makes it worthwhile.

TEMPERATURE
Day 70–85°F
Night 55–65°F

The related genera of *Catasetum*, *Clowesia*, *Cycnoches*, and *Mormodes* are found throughout the warm lowland tropical regions of Central and South America. Many of these plants are from areas with strong seasonal changes in rainfall; they are deciduous and require a rest period in winter with little or no water. While plants are in active growth, they perform best with warm temperatures.

LIGHT
Catasetum orchids enjoy bright light with minimal shading when they are in leaf. The thin leaves may seem delicate, but the plants need bright light to store up energy during their rapid growth in spring and summer before entering dormancy in the fall.

WATER
In this group of orchids, water must be applied at the right time during their spring and summer growth and nearly completely withheld during their dormant period, with only small amounts provided to prevent the pseudobulbs from shriveling. The temptation is to begin watering when the new leaves start to show in early summer after warm temperatures return, but it is best to wait for the new growth to be at least 3 to 4 inches long and starting to show new roots before starting to water. Early in the growth period, small amounts of water are cautiously added to keep water out of the new growth. As the growth increases in size, watering can be increased in frequency and quantity until the plants are being kept evenly moist as the growth nears maturity. Once the leaves begin to yellow and drop off, watering can be reduced; it

should be withheld when the leaves drop off the mature pseudobulbs as the plant enters the dry winter dormancy.

HUMIDITY

When *Catasetum* plants are in their dormancy, they can tolerate lower humidity (below 50%) with little or no issues. When the plants are actively growing in the warmer summer months, it is best to maintain humidity in the growing environment at 50% or higher to help the plants grow and prevent the outbreak of spider mites, a common pest of this group of orchids.

POTTING AND POTTING MIX

Catasetum orchids grow well in a fine bark mixture with added drainage for the rapidly growing root systems. Many growers report superb results planting in high-quality sphagnum moss, with the plants producing better growth and roots than in other potting mediums. Plants should be repotted shortly before they break their dormancy and the new shoots begin to grow.

FERTILIZER

Catasetum orchids are heavy feeders when they are in active growth. They appreciate regular watering and feeding with a full-strength balanced fertilizer every other watering. Once the plants have mature pseudobulbs, the feeding rate can be reduced and eventually stopped as the plants start to drop their leaves and enter dormancy for the winter.

PESTS AND DISEASES

Other than occasional outbreaks of aphids on new shoots, the main pests of *Catasetum* orchids are mites, particularly spider mites. These pests can be controlled with regular syringing of the foliage with a gentle shower of water and keeping humidity in the growing area elevated above 50% while the plants are in leaf.

CULTURE NOTES AND TIPS

- *Catasetum* orchids grow rapidly during the late spring through fall and require bright light and frequent watering and feeding to grow well. The treatment during the growing period will determine the quality and quantity of flowers produced the following season.
- Hold back on watering the plants until the new growth is at least 3 to 4 inches long and new roots can be seen on the base of the new shoot.
- Watch for spider mites when the plants are in leaf, and syringe the foliage with water to help avoid and control their populations.

Cattleya

The popularity of *Cattleya* orchids as hobbyist plants and corsage flowers have made them one of the most commonly cultivated groups of orchids around the world. Sometimes referred to as the Queen of Orchids for the large, colorful, and fragrant blooms, they have set the standard in horticulture since their introduction 200 years ago. Some horticulturists have focused on continuing to improve the natural forms of the species through line breeding exceptional plants, resulting in an increase in the quality and desired shape of the blooms. By selecting and breeding related genera of the *Cattleya* alliance, however, hybridizers have created a diverse range of plant sizes and flower colors, fragrances, and patterns. These complex hybrid genera have helped increase the diversity of *Cattleya* available to hobbyists and broadened their popularity over the years. Despite their complex pedigree, most of these plants grow and bloom well in a very similar range of conditions.

TEMPERATURE

Day 70–85°F
Night 55–65°F

Native to warm tropical forests in Central and South America, *Cattleya* is a durable and resilient genus that adapts to a range of warmer temperatures and conditions. Intermediate to warm conditions suit the plants best, with most varieties preferring warm temperatures consistently above 55°F. If you are able to provide a 10°F drop in temperatures between day and night, it greatly benefits the plants and encourages good growth and flowering. Temperatures above 85°F can be tolerated for short periods if the plants are not allowed to desiccate from lack of water or humidity and shade is provided to keep the foliage from overheating and burning. Many of the plants can tolerate cold conditions below 50°F, as long as they are not too wet and the new growth and leaves remain dry.

LIGHT

Cattleya orchids need long periods of bright indirect sunlight to grow and bloom well. Positioning the plants in a bright location is important, as lack of sunlight is one of the most common reasons for a lack of vigor and flowering. Bright light green foliage indicates the plants are getting proper light, and the pseudobulbs should be able to stand upright without much support. Dark green leaves and weak growth are often a sign of too little sunlight. In this case, the plants should be relocated to a better location or supplemental light added to the growing area for best blooming.

If the plant is being moved to a brighter location, protect the foliage with some initial shading or ease the plant into the new location to avoid burning the leaves, which can easily happen with a rapid increase in light levels.

WATER

Cattleya orchids appreciate regular watering year-round, as they do not have any seasonal dormancy. The thick leaves, coarse roots, and pseudobulbs store water, and allowing the plants to approach dryness between watering is encouraged. However, when the plants are producing new growth or expanding flower buds, they should not remain dry for too long. Water can be added to the surface of the potting medium, allowing it to flow freely through the container to provide aeration and moisture for the root system. When watering, try to keep water out of new growth and off flowers, as it can encourage bacterial or fungal diseases.

HUMIDITY

Humidity levels of 60–80% are best for the plants, as this replicates the forested environments where *Cattleya* orchids come from. Low humidity can be tolerated for short periods, but is best avoided, especially while the plants are developing flowers or are in bloom. As humidity increases, maintain buoyant air circulation around the plants to allow foliage and flowers to dry, which helps to prevent fungal diseases.

POTTING AND POTTING MIX

Cattleya orchids should be potted in a free-draining bark mix, which allows air around the coarse roots and water to move freely through the pots. Because most *Cattleya* are epiphytes, for good root growth they need an open potting medium that does not retain too much moisture. Many *Cattleya* have horizontally creeping rhizomes and need to be grown in short wide pots rather than narrow deep containers to afford room for the plants to grow. *Cattleya* orchids can also be grown mounted or in open baskets if ample humidity and water are provided. The plants should be repotted every 2 to 3 years or when the potting medium starts to break down.

FERTILIZER

Cattleya orchids require regular feeding, especially during their active growing season, which is usually spring to early summer. The plants should be fed regularly with a balanced fertilizer (20-20-20 or 20-10-20) at one-quarter the recommended label strength every second or third watering. This will help to build the strong growth and root systems necessary to produce and support the blooms. Some growers have had success with using small amounts of slow-release fertilizer (such as Osmocote or Nutricote) on more robust plants. Fertilizing should be decreased slightly in both frequency and concentration when the growth is fully mature or during winter, when light levels are lower and plants are not growing as quickly.

PESTS AND DISEASES

Common pests to watch for on *Cattleya* orchids include scale, mealybugs, thrips (especially on flowers), aphids, and slugs and snails.

CULTURE NOTES AND TIPS

- Repotting of plants is best done after flowering as the new growths have almost matured but before the new roots begin to show from the base of the new growth. Repotting at the wrong time of the year sometimes causes the plants to slow their growth and blooming.
- If you're unsure of the proper time to repot your plant, a good general rule is relatively soon after flowering.
- When repotting, try to disturb the roots as little as possible. This helps the plant recover and continue to grow after being divided or repotted.
- When dividing *Cattleya* plants, keep at least three or four pseudobulbs with healthy roots on each division to ensure they have enough reserves to continue growing.
- Keep water from sitting in or on new growth, flower sheaths, and open blooms to prevent them from rotting.

Cattleya Canhamiana 'Azure Skies'
C.

Originally bred and grown to provide June brides with cut flowers for their wedding bouquets, *Cattleya* Canhamiana is the result of crossing *Cattleya purpurata*, the immensely popular Brazilian species with a tremendous range of forms, and the large-flowered *Cattleya mossiae*, a parent of many of the large-flowered corsage-type *Cattleya* orchids. The resulting hybrid is a vigorous and floriferous plant and a reliable early-summer bloomer. In *C.* Canhamiana 'Azure Skies', the more uncommon coerulea or blue color forms were used by hybridizers looking to create smoky bluish purple flowers with a yellow throat. Thriving in bright light conditions, this hybrid will grow and multiply vigorously when well tended, quickly creating large specimen plants full of blooms.

Cattleya cernua

syn. *Sophronitis* cernua

C.

Native to southeastern Brazil, Paraguay, and Bolivia, this is one of the smallest members of the genus *Cattleya*, with tight creeping mats of hard oval leaves and barely resembling its larger cousins. What this plant doesn't have in size, however, it makes up for with long-lasting blooms of intense color. Crystalline scarlet orange blooms are produced in small clusters just above the foliage. In cultivation, *Cattleya cernua* prefers bright conditions and is a durable plant that tolerates a range of conditions. Over time, the plant will completely envelop a small basket or mount and produce multiple clusters of blooms at the same time.

Cattleya cernua bears starry, long-lasting orange red flowers on miniature plants.

Cattleya Dinard 'Blue Heaven'

syn. *Laeliocattleya* Dinard 'Blue Heaven'

C.

Pale blue or coerulea are the most elusive and prized shades found in *Cattleya* orchids. They occur naturally as rare mutations and in many cases can be difficult to create even by experienced breeders. Many of these blue-flowered rarities are not mass produced, so they are treasured and traded among serious collectors. *Cattleya* Dinard 'Blue Heaven' is one of the finer standard blues available. It is a strong cultivar producing fragrant blooms in unusual and elusive blue violet tones, with contrasting gold highlights on the lip. This plant provides a striking contrast to the more typical pink and white flowers more commonly encountered in orchid collections.

Cattleya Drumbeat 'Heritage'

syn. *Laeliocattleya* Drumbeat 'Heritage'
C.

Cattleya Drumbeat 'Heritage' is an excellent and reliable spring-blooming orchid with lavender pink flowers. A very vigorous and prolific bloomer, this cattleya is a classic flower with regard to form, size, and fragrance. The large ruffled pink bloom is the embodiment of what many people think of as an orchid flower. Created by the famous Stewart Orchids in the late 1960s, this plant has definitely stood the test of time.

Cattleya 'Drumbeat 'Heritage' is an heirloom hybrid that is a reliable spring bloomer.

Cattleya Mari's Song

syn. *Laeliocattleya* Mari's Song
C.

Occasionally during breeding, orchids can mutate and produce colors and patterns that are atypical. The normally drab petals can suddenly develop patterns similar to those on the lip or labellum. This type of chance mutation is technically a peloric flower, but hobbyists collectively refer to them as Splash Petal cattleyas. Many of these plants breed true to type and are used to create wildly patterned blooms with bars, stripes, and flares on the flowers. *Cattleya* Mari's Song has light pink flowers splashed with magenta-red and yellow and a strong fragrance similar to tea rose. The plants are compact and floriferous, blooming in late spring to early summer.

Cattleya Melody Fair 'Carol'

syn. *Brassolaeliocattleya* Melody Fair 'Carol'
C.

Orchid hybridizers have created a huge range of colors and patterns over the years. Flowers with white sepals and petals with a colored or patterned labellum are defined as "semi-alba," referring to the partially white bloom. For many years, this pattern was very popular with breeders whose goal was to intensify and saturate the color on the labellum. *Cattleya* Melody Fair 'Carol' is considered by collectors to be one of the finest of its type, with a sharp contrast of the pristine white flower and the deeply saturated magenta purple labellum further enhanced by a faint white picotee along the ruffled edges of the lip. This hybrid is a reliable winter to early spring bloomer.

Cattleya Mini Purple

syn. *Laeliocattleya* Mini Purple
C.

The large flowers on compact plants make *Cattleya* Mini Purple an excellent choice for small spaces.

The genus *Cattleya* offers a tremendous range of colors, sizes, and fragrances to orchid breeders. While for many years the large ruffled blooms of corsage-type *Cattleya* orchids seemed to dominate the interests of hybridizers, many have turned their efforts to breed compact plants with all the color, fragrance, and classic look of their larger cousins. With an enormous diversity of colors and shapes, one could build a collection of "mini-catts" alone. *Cattleya* Mini Purple is a standout bred from two diminutive Brazilian species. The 3- to 4-inch light to magenta purple blooms are almost as large as the plant and put on quite a show in a small space. The plants perform best in a well-drained mix with plenty of sunlight and water when they are actively growing.

Cattlianthe Gold Digger 'Fuchs Mandarin'

syn. *Laeliocattleya* Gold Digger 'Fuchs Mandarin'

Ctt.

Some breeders have moved away from the large blousy blooms of standard *Cattleya* orchids and focused on producing plants that are strong growers and prolific bloomers, with clusters of smaller but no less impressive flowers. One of the best of these types is *Cattlianthe* Gold Digger 'Fuchs Mandarin', a regular showstopper at spring exhibitions. The 3-inch-wide glowing tangerine flowers with maroon spots are produced in dense clusters, with up to a dozen blooms, at the top of the pseudobulb from late winter to early spring. This variety is tolerant of a wide range of temperatures and conditions, making it an ideal plant for either a windowsill or even outdoors in warm climates.

Masses of golden orange blooms are reliably produced every spring to early summer on *Cattlianthe* Gold Digger 'Fuchs Mandarin'.

Cattlianthe Jewel Box 'Scheherazade'

syn. *Sophrolaeliocattleya* Jewel Box 'Scheherazade'

Ctt.

Cattlianthe Jewel Box is a perennial favorite among orchid growers and collectors. Although the flowers lack fragrance, the plant more than makes up for it by reliably producing clusters of four to ten bright red 3-inch blooms above the compact growth every year from late winter to early spring. Plants produce multiple leads quickly and grow well even in slightly lower light conditions than most cattleyas would enjoy. Specimen plants with dozens of flowers are a common sight at spring orchid shows, attracting admirers new and old for this classic hybrid.

Cattlianthe Jewel Box 'Scheherazade' produces bright red clusters of blooms.

Clowesia Rebecca Northen 'Pink Grapefruit'
Clo.

An unusual but beautiful orchid that is deserving of greater popularity, *Clowesia* Rebecca Northen is named after a historic author and great champion of growing orchids in the home. This orchid is naturally deciduous, dropping the pleated leaves during a winter rest period each year. As the plant begins to resume growth in spring, it produces short chains of shell-shaped blooms around the base of the plant that often cascade over the edge of the pot. The light pink blooms have a fringed and fuzzy lip, adding to their charm and character. When the plants are in active growth, they require regular watering and feeding for the pseudobulbs to mature. As the leaves start to yellow, withhold watering and only mist the plant slightly to prevent pseudobulbs from shriveling completely. It's a challenge not to water or fuss over the plant while it is dormant, but your patience will be rewarded with many spikes of flowers as the plant resumes its growth with the onset of spring and summer.

Cascades of fragrant pink blooms are produced around the base of the deciduous plants of *Clowesia* Rebecca Northen.

Cymbidium

Cymbidium orchids have been enjoying a recent surge in popularity as plants have become more available in the market and breeders have introduced compact, warmth-tolerant, floriferous plants with long-lasting sprays of blooms. *Cymbidium* orchids are among the first orchids to have been cultivated for their delicate sprays of fragrant blooms. Many of the larger hybrids needed cold conditions to trigger flower buds to develop, and the plants required enormous amounts of space to grow and bloom. These are still widely cultivated in areas where they can be grown outdoors for much of the year, and only recently have newer hybrids been created for the indoor gardener.

TEMPERATURE
Day 65–85°F
Night 50–65°F

Cymbidium orchids have an extremely wide distribution, ranging from northern India into China and Japan and south throughout the Pacific Islands and into Australia. They grow both terrestrially and as epiphytes. Many *Cymbidium* species are found in regions where winter temperatures can approach freezing and the summers are warm with frequent rains. The plants can tolerate a wide range of temperatures and are popular subjects for outdoor growing where mild winters occur. In the garden, greenhouse, or home, duplicating seasonal changes in water and temperature help the plants flower profusely and grow vigorously.

LIGHT
Cymbidium orchids require strong light to grow well. The plants can be grown in full sun, and the foliage should be a bright yellow green, showing that the plants are getting enough sunlight. When temperatures are consistently above 50°F, plants do well outdoors with minimal shade and they appreciate the added sunlight. In the summer, plants should be placed in the shade of trees or protected from the most intense sunlight during the warmest time of the day to prevent burning of the foliage.

WATER
Even though *Cymbidium* orchids have pseudobulbs for water storage and large coarse root systems, these semi-terrestrial orchids prefer even moisture during the growing period. When the plants are actively growing in the spring and early summer, they should receive regular and frequent watering to maintain their long leaves. The plants can be kept slightly drier during the cooler temperature of fall and winter, when the plants are slowing down and getting ready to produce their flower spikes.

HUMIDITY

During spring and summer, the plants benefit from medium to high humidity, with a minimum of 50% relative humidity preferred. A higher than average humidity also helps to suppress the spread of spider mites, one of the more common pests of *Cymbidium* foliage.

POTTING AND POTTING MIX

Cymbidium orchids are semi-terrestrial plants, and they do well in a fine bark mix in large containers to accommodate the vigorous root systems. Some growers add chunky peat moss or even a portion of soilless potting mix such as ProMix to the bark mixtures to help with water retention and good root growth. Repotting is best done when the new growth begins shortly after flowering. For the best flowering, the plants should be repotted every 2 to 3 years and the roots allowed to become pot bound.

FERTILIZER

Cymbidium orchids are very heavy feeders when the plants are in active growth. Weekly applications of full-strength balanced fertilizers help the plants produce strong growth and store up the energy needed to produce the spring floral displays they are prized for. Cymbidiums are one of the few groups of orchids that appreciate slow-release fertilizers (such as Osmocote and Nutricote) to help supply the large amounts of food they need. As the fall approaches and temperatures drop, reduce feeding and watering as the plants slow their growth.

PESTS AND DISEASES

Cymbidium hybrids are relatively pest free but can become infested with scale or spider mites on the pseudobulbs and foliage. Regular inspections and grooming of dead and dying leaves are helpful to remove any hiding places for insects and find infestations before they get out of hand. Regular syringing of the foliage with water of the foliage helps to prevent spider mites by dislodging them and raises the humidity around the plants. Aphids are a common pest, especially during the bloom season; they should be treated immediately because they can rapidly damage flowers and spread the viruses that commonly infect *Cymbidium*.

CULTURE NOTES AND TIPS

- *Cymbidium* orchids prefer strong sunlight and generous applications of water and fertilizer to grow and bloom their best.
- These are vigorous plants and benefit from repotting every 2 to 3 years. Allow them to become slightly pot bound for best flowering.
- Many *Cymbidium* orchids require cold night temperatures in the range of 45–55°F to set and develop flower buds in the fall to early winter. If temperatures are too warm, the plants will not bloom properly.

Cymbidium Compact Hybrids
Cym.

Most standard *Cymbidium* hybrids are large and require a tremendous amount of space to accommodate the plant and its flower spikes, which in some cases can be nearly 5 feet long. Despite their beauty and long-lasting blooms, many people just don't have the space available. Hybridizers have focused on making compact versions of standard cymbidiums with all the color and fragrance on a smaller floriferous plant. These recent introductions have been bred with Chinese and Japanese species to create more warmth-tolerant, compact, and easily reblooming plants without the cold period required by most standard cymbidium hybrids. *Cymbidium* Enzan Current 'Aquarius', *Cymbidium* Lovely Moon 'Crescent', and *Cymbidium* Royal Red 'Princess Nobuko' are new Japanese hybrids that have captured the interest of orchid enthusiasts and collectors.

Cymbidium Dorothy Stockstill 'Forgotten Fruit'
Cym.

One of the trends in modern *Cymbidium* breeding is the use of the unusual species *Cymbidium devonianum* to impart warmth tolerance, create graceful cascading flower spikes, and give satin textures to the flowers. The species has olive green and purple flowers that by some standards would seem almost drab, but as a parent it imparts fantastic rich colors into its progeny. One of the most successful of this group of hybrids is *Cymbidium* Dorothy Stockstill 'Forgotten Fruit', a plant that embodies all of the best qualities of this line of breeding. When healthy, this warm-tolerant floriferous hybrid rings the base of the plant with velvet-textured flowers in dark reds, looking more like luscious berries than flowers. Compared to most standard *Cymbidium* orchids, it is a relatively compact plant with 24-inch foliage.

Cymbidium Golden Elf
Cym.

Chinese *Cymbidium* species have been relatively ignored by hybridizers, who were much more focused on colorful and large-flowered standard *Cymbidium* orchids. A few intrepid breeders started incorporating some of these graceful species known for their powerful and pleasing fragrances into new lines of breeding and achieved some fantastic initial results. *Cymbidium* Golden Elf retained the upright flower spikes from the Chinese species *Cymbidium ensifolium* and the powerful sweet fragrance. The narrow graceful foliage shows off the tall spikes of chrome yellow flowers borne in profusion every spring to early summer. A compact grower and perhaps one of the most warmth tolerant of all *Cymbidium* hybrids, the plant even grows and blooms well in warm areas such as Florida, where standard *Cymbidium* plants notoriously refuse to grow.

Cymbidium Golden Elf is a highly fragrant, compact plant that, unlike other cymbidiums, will tolerate hot humid conditions.

Cymbidium Sara Jean 'Ice Cascade'
Cym.

One of the best and most floriferous of all miniature *Cymbidium* hybrids, *Cymbidium* Sara Jean 'Ice Cascade' is a plant that no enthusiast should be without. On this 24-inch-tall plant with compact pseudobulbs and growth, it's not uncommon to see specimens completely ringed with fragrant white and pale yellow blooms in late winter to spring. The upright foliage allows the flowers to gracefully cascade over the edge of the pot. The plant can be grown on top of a bench during most of the year and then hung to allow the flowers to develop and display to their best. Although this hybrid is warmth tolerant, the best display of blooms comes after providing cool nighttime temperatures in the 50–60°F range.

Hard Cane Dendrobiums

The genus *Dendrobium* is one of the largest and most diverse groups of orchids in the world, with several hundred species ranging in size from tiny miniatures to giants with pseudobulbs reaching over 7 feet tall. The plants are mainly epiphytes in nature, and many have long-lasting colorful blooms, traits appreciated by both hybridizers and orchid enthusiasts. Sometimes called hard cane *Dendrobium*, the two sections most commonly encountered are Phaleananthe *Dendrobium*, named for the resemblance of the blooms to those of *Phalaenopsis*, and Spatulata *Dendrobium*, often called antelope dendrobiums because the petals are elongated and spirally twisted like the horns of many antelope. Within these sections of *Dendrobium*, hybridizers have created an extensive range of selections for the pot plant and cut flower industry. They are still popular subjects for orchid growers, especially in warm tropical regions, for their free-flowering habit and colorful blooms.

TEMPERATURE

Day 70–85°F

Night 60–68°F

The species used in hybridizing hard cane dendrobiums are found across the Pacific Islands, Indonesia, New Guinea, and into Australia. Many of these large epiphytic plants grow at or near sea level with hot and humid conditions year-round. Because the plants do not experience low temperatures or much of a seasonal change in their natural habitat, hard cane dendrobiums can bloom nearly year-round when provided with similar temperatures and conditions. If the plants are exposed to temperatures below 60°F even for short periods, many will drop their leaves, making the plants appear as if they are dead or dying. The canes will remain bare until new growth brings new leaves after warm temperatures return.

LIGHT

This particular group of *Dendrobium* prefers very bright light to grow and flower well. The plants are often found growing in full sun, even in the tropics, and thrive in light levels that would burn most other orchids. High light conditions will even cause a slight purple or red tint to the foliage, which is not harmful but a reaction to strong sunlight. If hard cane dendrobiums are grown in shady low light conditions, the growth and foliage will be weak and soft and often more susceptible to disease and leaf spotting.

WATER

When actively growing, *Dendrobium* orchids like regular and heavy watering to help the new growths expand and mature. They prefer to be pot bound and well drained. Allow them to dry slightly at the roots between watering.

HUMIDITY

Dendrobium orchids prefer high humidity, similar to the warm tropical environments where they are native. Constant humidity of over 50% is preferred, but the plants can tolerate dry conditions when the new growth has matured or during the cooler months of the year.

POTTING AND POTTING MIX

Dendrobium orchids are not too fussy about their potting medium, growing well in a variety of substrates. Orchid mixes containing bark, charcoal, perlite, and even sphagnum suit the fine roots well, as long as they are well drained. Stagnant mixes or mixes that have broken down can suffocate the fine roots of the plants. Many *Dendrobium* orchids prefer to be pot bound and do well in small pots relative to the size of the plants. Growing them in too large of a pot often results in a decrease in vigor and problems with the roots.

FERTILIZER

When in active growth during the warmer months of the year, *Dendrobium* orchids are heavy feeders and enjoy regular applications of balanced fertilizer at one-half to full strength every other watering. Some growers use slow-release fertilizers (such as Osmocote or Nutricote) in small amounts. Fertilizer should be reduced in frequency and concentration once the growth has matured.

PESTS AND DISEASES

Dendrobiums are subject to many of the same pests and diseases that bother other orchids. Aphids are drawn to new growths and tender new buds and flower spikes. Mealybugs and scale insects are found on succulent new growths, and fungal diseases can attack soft new foliage.

CULTURE NOTES AND TIPS

- Native to warm tropical regions of the world, *Dendrobium* orchids require warm conditions above 60°F for best growth and flowering. Even a short chill below 60°F can cause plants to rapidly drop foliage, leaving the canes bare. New foliage will return only when plants are returned to the proper temperature range.
- Constant bright light and warm temperatures are the foundations for success for this group of orchids.
- *Dendrobium* orchids prefer to be pot bound. Keeping them in small pots helps to promote the best growth and flowering.
- Try to keep water off foliage, especially after nightfall, as some *Dendrobium* hybrids can be prone to leaf spotting.

Dendrobium Hard Cane Type Hybrids
Den.

Hard Cane type *Dendrobium* hybrids offer a tremendous range of sizes, colors, flower patterns, and even now miniature varieties for the orchid hobbyist. *Dendrobium* Burana Jade has light minty green flowers, *Dendrobium* Burana Sapphire bears saturated violet blue flowers, and *Dendrobium* Emma White has creamy white blooms. These orchids prefer warm temperatures throughout the year, and even short periods below 60°F will result in leaf drop. When the plants are cultivated with bright light and regular feeding, they can produce sprays of long-lasting colorful blooms multiple times during the year. When healthy, the plants are durable and long-lived specimens.

TOP Modern *Dendrobium* hybrids have been created with combinations of colors and patterns beyond what is found in nature, such as the pink-brushed green flowers of *Dendrobium* Burana 'Emerald'.

MIDDLE Another popular pattern is flowers that are striped with contrasting colors like the bright candy-striped flowers of *Dendrobium* Burana Stripe.

BOTTOM The dark velvet maroon blooms of *Dendrobium* Quique Ramirez 'Karen's Delight' make a striking display.

Green is one of the more popular and unusual flower colors in dendrobiums, as seen in *Dendrobium* Burana Green 'First Chance'.

Dendrobium Enobi Purple 'Splash'
Den.

Orchid breeders often spend years trying to achieve a certain color pattern or flower shape. But sometimes a chance mutation occurs, creating a seedling that is completely new and unexpected. The unusual flower pattern mutation of *Dendrobium* Enobi Purple 'Splash' appeared in a Taiwanese orchid breeder's collection, and thankfully someone noticed and propagated it. The plants are profuse bloomers, with flowers appearing several times a year on compact plants under 12 inches tall. The unique flowers have a crystalline white base and magenta patterning on the sepals and petals, looking like someone brushed them with paint. The hybrid was originally bred using a dwarf form of the Australian *Dendrobium bigibbum* to create compact floriferous plants. Since its introduction, this hybrid has received considerable and well-deserved attention from the orchid-growing community.

The unusually patterned blooms of *Dendrobium* Enobi Purple 'Splash' are the result of a chance discovery in a group of plants.

Dendrobium Frosty Dawn
Den.

This delightful hybrid is bred from several species in the Nigrohirsute section of *Dendrobium*, named for the distinctive short black hairs on the pseudobulbs and new growth. This group has become popular with hybridizers for their long-lasting and sometimes fragrant flowers that are produced along the length of the pseudobulbs in spring to summer each year. The waxy white, cream, or green sepals and petals of *Dendrobium* Frosty Dawn provide a perfect background for the fiery red orange lip. The 1-inch flowers are produced in small clusters along the non-deciduous stems and are produced profusely when the plants are happy. This hybrid prefers bright direct light and warm conditions and does not require a seasonal rest period to initiate flowers.

Dendrobium kingianum

Den.

Australia is home to many *Dendrobium* species that have become very popular with orchidists the world around. These species are often found growing on rocks in exposures ranging from partial shade to full blazing sun and can experience both extreme heat and cold without damage. As a result, they are absolutely durable, hardy, and forgiving plants for the orchid grower. The spindle-shaped pseudobulbs of *Dendrobium kingianum* form dense clusters with a few leathery oval leaves at their tips. The highly fragrant ½-inch flowers are borne in profusion just above the foliage; on well-grown specimens, they can almost obscure the foliage in a haze of strongly perfumed blooms. This species has been hybridized extensively with related species. The Australian species and their hybrids have a dedicated group of admirers and deserve to be more widely cultivated for their fragrance, profuse flowering habit, and ease of culture.

Dendrobium Micro Chip

Den.

The miniature species *Dendrobium aberrans* was used in the breeding of *Dendrobium* Micro Chip. Despite the parent plant being a challenge for some, this and the other hybrids have been quite the opposite. These compact plants can produce dozens of white to cream flowers spotted purple and can easily fill out a 4-inch pot in no time at all. The long-lasting flowers look good for up to 3 or 4 months under ideal conditions, making them floriferous and impressive specimens despite their small size. The plants grow well alongside *Paphiopedilum* and *Phalaenopsis* and are easy to grow and flower under most conditions.

Nobile Dendrobiums

Within the genus *Dendrobium*, there is an extraordinary diversity of plant types and forms. Nobile dendrobiums are distributed throughout much of Southeast Asia and north into India and the Himalayas. Many of the species closely related to and resembling *Dendrobium nobile*, including the yellow *Dendrobium heterocarpum* and pink *Dendrobium regium*, have been interbred to increase the range of flower color and pattern within this group. Flowers with reds, oranges, yellow, white, and magenta pink, with many possessing a contrasting dark spot of color on the lip, have been created by hybridizers. Nobile dendrobiums are prized for brightly colored and sweetly fragrant flowers, which cover the soft canes with blooms and give the effect of a dense bouquet of flowers. Their cultural requirements are different from many of the other commonly cultivated dendrobiums, so they are treated here as a separate group of plants. Despite their reputation for being challenging to grow and rebloom, the floral display that these plants create is worth every extra bit of effort.

TEMPERATURE
Day 70–80°F for most of the year
Night 55–65°F

Many of the species used to breed this group of hybrids are native to areas where there are marked differences in temperature and rainfall between seasons. They experience cool to cold, dry winters with little or no rainfall and summers that are warm and wet. As a result, nobile dendrobiums need a cooler dry dormancy to trigger the flower buds to develop in spring. Many of the plants also become partially to completely deciduous, dropping their leaves in winter. During their winter rest period, the plants should be kept cooler during the day and night, with temperatures below 70°F if possible.

LIGHT
Like many *Dendrobium* hybrids, this group of plants prefers bright light conditions. The leaves should be a bright grass green, not dark green. Strong light promotes strong upright stems and good growth, which will encourage profuse flowering.

WATER
When the plants are in active growth, they prefer to be kept evenly moist and appreciate only drying slightly between watering. One special requirement, however, is that in late fall and winter watering should be reduced to nearly stopped. As difficult as this might sound, only water or mist the plants to prevent the pseudobulbs from

shriveling. Nobile dendrobiums are adapted to sometimes going months without any significant amount of water. The plants will drop some foliage, but this is completely normal.

HUMIDITY

Nobile dendrobiums need at least 50% humidity when the plants are growing. Low humidity can sometimes result in problems with new foliage and even encourage spider mites to infest the soft new leaves.

POTTING AND POTTING MIX

Like most *Dendrobium* orchids, nobile dendrobiums prefer to be pot bound and do well in small containers. The plants do well in any medium that is free draining and allows their vigorous fine root systems to develop and grow. Fine bark mixtures or sphagnum moss are good choices.

FERTILIZER

When they are in active growth after flowering, nobile dendrobiums require regular feeding with a one-half strength balanced fertilizer. Applying a high-nitrogen fertilizer often results in new growth and keikis (small plantlets) rather than flowers. As autumn approaches, it is best to stop fertilizing and allow the plants to enter their rest period. While the plants are dormant, do not fertilize them.

PESTS AND DISEASES

Common pests that attack nobile dendrobiums include aphids and thrips, which enjoy the new foliage and flower buds. Spider mites can become a problem if the environment has constant low humidity. The foliage of nobile dendrobiums can be infected with fungal leaf spotting if the plants are watered or allowed to remain wet after dark.

CULTURE NOTES AND TIPS

- These semi-deciduous orchids require a dormancy period from fall through winter, when water and fertilizer should be withheld and the plants kept cool and dry. If not allowed to lie dormant, the plants will not flower.
- Water and feed while in active growth, but avoid high concentrations of fertilizers as fall approaches.

Dendrobium Roy Tokunaga

Den.

A few intrepid hybridizers have been breeding orchids within the Latouria section of *Dendrobium* that is native to New Guinea and surrounding islands. They are characterized by long-lasting green to cream flowers, often with spots and bright patterns on the lip, produced just above the compact canes. One of the most successful of this group of hybrids is *Dendrobium* Roy Tokunaga. The 12- to 18-inch-tall plants bear a profusion of creamy white blooms with a light green lip, with much of the flower spotted and barred with purple. The plants continue to produce flower spikes even from older canes and can make specimens with hundreds of blooms in just a few years. Latouria hybrids are intermediate- to warm-growing plants with no distinct rest period, so they should receive water and fertilizer year-round. They grow and flower best when the root system becomes pot bound.

Dendrobium Samurai

Den.

Antelope dendrobiums are known as such because their flowers have upright twisted petals that resemble the spiral horns of many antelope species. These hybrids are popular in warm tropical regions as profusely flowering landscape plants. Some antelope dendrobiums get enormous, with single canes reaching 6 feet tall or more. Others are more compact, such as *Dendrobium* Samurai, whose petals appear to defy gravity while spiraling upward from the white flowers with and pink-striped lips. This free-flowering hybrid needs very bright light and warm conditions to perform best.

Dendrobium spectabile
Den.

This orchid is often described as looking more like something from the bottom of the sea rather than a tropical jungle. *Dendrobium spectabile* is native to New Guinea and the surrounding islands and is a delightful oddity to add to any orchid collection. This robust plant produces pseudobulbs up to 24 inches high. The long-lasting flowers never fail to attract attention. The 3-inch undulating and twisted pale yellow green blooms are striped and spotted rust red and produced in a cluster just above the foliage. *Dendrobium spectabile* grows and blooms well in bright light and warm conditions.

Dendrochilum magnum
Ddc.

The genus *Dendrochilum* is a large and varied one, with many species worthy of horticultural praise. These orchids are neat clumping plants that often bloom in profusion with each new flush of growth. Many of the species are characterized by long hanging chains of tiny fragrant flowers, like *Dendrochilum magnum*, one of the largest of the species in cultivation. This species is native to the Philippines and is a reliable fall bloomer with acid green flowers that age to copper orange. The plant's arching spiral inflorescences can put on quite a show, despite the individual blooms being less than ½ inch in diameter. The flowers have a strong citrus or cedar fragrance that can fill a room, adding to the overall display. The vigorous clumping plants do well in potting mixes suitable for paphiopedilums, with small bark suitable for their fine root systems. Even moisture throughout the growing season and regular feeding helps this species develop into a specimen quickly.

TOP The twisted blooms of *Dendrobium spectabile* are some of the more bizarre-looking orchid flowers.

BOTTOM The small individual blooms of *Dendrochilum magnum* peek out from the bracts on the graceful, long hanging chains of flowers.

Encyclia cordigera
E.

This South American species has long been popular with orchid collectors for the upright flower spikes with several highly fragrant flowers. Each of the flowers has a striking color combination, with undulating dark brown sepals and petals with a bright magenta purple lip. Even out of bloom, the polished pseudobulbs with rigid foliage are attractive and interesting. *Encyclia cordigera* is a durable and forgiving species that grows well alongside *Cattleya*, which is a close relative. Even moisture during the growing season and bright light help this plant produce strong clumps of growth that will produce multiple flower spikes at once, making an impressive display of color and fragrance.

Encyclia cordigera bears brightly colored and strongly fragrant blooms.

Epidendrum peperomia
Epi.

This delightful miniature species is native to Colombia and Venezuela. Despite taxonomists changing the official name of this species a number of times over the past several years, what has not changed are the many delightful qualities of this miniature orchid. The low creeping mat of alternating ovate foliage can develop a red maroon cast in high light conditions. In spring to early summer, the curious flowers dot the surface of this tufted plant, with each bloom held just above the foliage. The individual flowers have thin light green sepals and petals offset by a prominent glossy maroon lip that looks like the shell of a beetle or other insect perched on the foliage. Although the flowers are relatively small, their high-gloss shine sets them off against the foliage, and the mass of blooms produced on a well-grown plant make for a handsome display. The miniature plants do best with even moisture and ample humidity throughout the year to prevent the fine root systems from drying out.

The whimsical flowers of *Epidendrum peperomia* resemble insects resting on the foliage.

Fredclarkeara After Dark
Fdk.

The concept of a black orchid was always something of a literary fantasy until hybridizers started breeding with a group of related Central and South American orchid genera. This hybrid, which includes *Catasetum, Clowesia,* and *Mormodes* in its pedigree, is one of the darkest orchid hybrids produced to date. Through selective breeding, the hybridizer succeeded in creating a plant that produces blooms of such a dark maroon that they appear black. *Fredclarkeara* After Dark has rocketed in popularity for its exotic and almost unbelievable flower color. The plants require some more exacting conditions, with a seasonal dormancy during which they require little or no moisture to succeed. While in active growth, the plants need regular water and frequent feedings to get the best growth and eventual blooming. They produce broad thin foliage that is attractive to some plant pests, especially spider mites, which can cause extensive damage if not quickly eradicated.

Fredclarkeara After Dark is one of the blackest orchid flowers created by hybridizers to date.

Gastrochilus retrocalla
syn. *Haraella retrocalla*
Gchls.

This tiny epiphytic species native to Taiwan produces a fan of leaves that's less than 3 inches in diameter. Despite the small habit, the cheerful yellow and maroon blooms are nearly as large as the plant and appear in succession over a short period in late winter and spring. The tiny fragrant flowers resemble a little bumble bee, and this orchid always gets a smile out of viewers when it is in bloom. The truly miniature plants can be grown in a small pot or as a mounted specimen at intermediate temperatures with year-round watering.

Guaritonia Why Not
syn. *Cattleytonia* Why Not
Grt.

As the story goes, the hybridizer who pondered the possible hybrid between a miniature magenta-flowered Jamaican species and a larger bright orange Central American species looked at the two plants in flower and thought "Why not?" The resulting hybrid was not only surprising but also considered to have inherited the best of both parents. *Guaritonia* Why Not, with free-flowering ruby red clusters of miniature blooms with a bright golden disk on the center of the lip, immediately became popular with orchid growers. The compact plants—often less than 12 inches tall—are floriferous and are perfect for someone looking for lots of color in an orchid that takes up little space. They grow well in similar conditions as required by cattleyas and are reliable bloomers in spring to early summer.

The bright blooms on miniature plants make *Guaritonia* Why Not a perfect choice for growers with limited space.

Jewel Orchids

This group of unusual and sometimes related orchids has evolved leaves with patterns and colors that allow them to be camouflaged on the forest floor and hidden from herbivores. Jewel orchids are prized by collectors for their intricately patterned and colored foliage more than the blooms of the plants. The many jewel orchids from around the world all grow in leaf litter on the forest floor in low light and humid conditions. These miniature to compact plants are prized and easy subjects for the orchid collector. They do well in terrariums, where many different varieties can happily coexist in a small space.

TEMPERATURE
Day 70–85°F
Night 60–68°F

Jewel orchids are found on the shaded forest floors of both temperate and tropical forests of the world. Most of the cultivated species are from lowland rainforests of Southeast Asia and the Pacific Islands, where they grow as terrestrial plants in low-light, warm, and humid conditions. If conditions become cool and dry, some species drop their leaves and go through a brief dormancy, surviving on the stored reserves in their succulent stems until warmth and moisture return. To keep the plants continually producing the leaves they treasured for, jewel orchids are best grown in intermediate to warm temperatures throughout the year.

LIGHT
Jewel orchids grow best in low light conditions, and they do well in east-facing or even bright north-facing windows. The plants are light sensitive, and the delicate leaves burn easily in high light or bright light conditions. Keep the plants shaded year-round, and watch them carefully for signs of too much light.

WATER
These orchids have succulent stems and leaves that provide some protection against drying out, but they do prefer even moisture to grow well. Drying out for any length of time causes the plants to drop their foliage and in some cases go dormant, leaving only a thin worm-like stem to resprout leaves when favorable conditions return. Jewel orchids appreciate regular misting and watering, and many prefer soft water without dissolved minerals to produce the best quality leaves.

HUMIDITY

Native to shady humid environments on the forest floor, jewel orchids need constant humidity above 60% as they have only small succulent stems for protection against dry desiccating conditions. Unlike most orchids, the plants are best grown in a terrarium to help provide the humidity they need year-round.

POTTING AND POTTING MIX

These terrestrial orchids grow best in sphagnum moss or peat-based soilless mixes with some perlite or sponge rock for added drainage. They are relatively accepting of any free-draining mix as long as it is kept evenly moist and not allowed to dry out.

FERTILIZER

Jewel orchids are not heavy feeders and prefer dilute amounts of fertilizer applied infrequently for the best growth. Using a balanced fertilizer at one-quarter the recommended label strength applied once a month is fine.

PESTS AND DISEASES

Jewel orchids can be attractive to mealybugs and spider mites, especially in less than ideal conditions when the plants are under stress. If ideal growing conditions are maintained, the plants can remain relatively pest free. Some of the most problematic pests of jewel orchids are slugs and snails, which find the succulent foliage attractive; if not noticed, they can destroy a plant in short time.

CULTURE NOTES AND TIPS

- Cultivate jewel orchids in shady humid conditions out of direct sunlight.
- Jewel orchids thrive in terrariums, where many other orchids do not.
- Good-quality water and even humidity are best.
- Many growers pinch off developing flower spikes to encourage stronger growth and increase foliage.
- Jewel orchids can be easily rooted from stem cuttings. As the plants get larger, they can be separated or sections of the creeping stems used to propagate new plants.

Jewel Orchids

Collectors treasure jewel orchids for their beautifully marked and veined foliage, which the plants have evolved to camouflage themselves among the leaf litter to avoid herbivores. Although jewel orchid species are distributed around the world and have a diverse range of sizes, colors, and patterns, they all share similar cultivation requirements: medium to low light, even moisture, and high humidity. Some of the best selections for the home orchid grower are *Ludisia discolor*, which has dark velvet black leaves with red veins, *Macodes petola*, with light green leaves laced with golden sparking veins, and *Anoectochilus formosanus* with dark green leaves and a network of gold veins.

Leomesezia Lava Burst 'Puanani'
syn. *Howeara* Lava Burst
Leom.

Bred from genera within the *Oncidium* Alliance, *Leomesezia* Lava Burst 'Puanani' is a delightful little hybrid that produces a profusion of bright red and orange flowers from many spikes. The plants are quick growers, creating compact clumps of narrow 8-inch leaves borne atop small clustered pseudobulbs, making specimens with many blooms in short time. The plants enjoy bright light and warm temperatures, but they do appreciate drying slightly between watering. This little plant certainly packs some impressive flower power in a small space.

TOP *Ludisia discolor* is one of the easiest of all jewel orchids to grow. It thrives in lower light conditions, making it a good companion for houseplants such as African violets.

BOTTOM *Macodes petola*, with intricately veined foliage, is best grown in a terrarium.

Leptotes bicolor

Lpt.

This is a small epiphytic species from Brazil. Eventually making a dense cluster over time, the thin pendant terete foliage is itself attractive. *Leptotes bicolor* blooms reliably and profusely in late winter to early spring, with small clusters of pristine white flowers offset with a magenta blotch on the lip. This orchid does well mounted or in small pots. Although it is tolerant of a wide range of temperatures and conditions, this species grows best in intermediate to warm conditions. *Leptotes bicolor* easily makes a showy floriferous specimen plant in short time and in a small space.

Lockhartia oerstedii

Lhta.

This unusual member of the *Oncidium* Alliance is distributed from Mexico to Panama and into Colombia. It is grown for the beautiful arching stems of imbricated foliage that give the entire plant a braided appearance. It blooms periodically throughout the year with small bright yellow flowers spotted with rusty red orange. The plant's numerous individual stems can continually produce flowers for many years. *Lockhartia oerstedii* produces

Leptotes bicolor is floriferous and easy to grow in a basket or on a mount.

many small plantlets that can be removed and planted when they develop a root system. Since the plant does not possess much ability to store water, it's best too keep it evenly moist and not allow it to dry out for long periods. *Lockhartia oerstedii* is a vigorous species that will happily grow in the same conditions favored by *Paphiopedilum* and *Phalaenopsis*.

Masdevallia

This genus of jewel-like compact to miniature orchids from the cloud forests of Central and South America has long been popular with enthusiasts despite a reputation for being challenging. The colorful triangular and tailed flowers are produced in profusion. The plants do well in lower light and cool temperatures, making them excellent choices for those with limited space or cooler conditions year-round. Hybridizers continue to work to improve the color range, patterns, and warmth tolerance of *Masdevallia* hybrids to make them more accessible to orchid enthusiasts and not just the serious orchid collector.

TEMPERATURE
Day 65–75°F
Night 55–60°F

Many wild species of *Masdevallia* are native to cloud forests, where the plants experience near constant cool temperatures with abundant moisture throughout the year. When grown in areas with hot humid summers, the plants quickly decline and die if temperatures are over 85°F for long periods of time. However, hybridizers have selectively bred plants to create hybrids that are more tolerant of warm temperatures, helping to make *Masdevallia* orchids more amenable to home gardeners.

LIGHT
Masdevallia species are native to cool shaded cloud forests and most experience dappled diffuse sunlight, making the selections suitable for lower light conditions. They grow well alongside other lower light orchids such as *Paphiopedilum* and are adaptable to growing under artificial lights or terrarium conditions.

WATER
Many *Masdevallia* hybrids can be sensitive to water with a high mineral content and other dissolved materials, so they need a constant supply of good-quality water all year-round. The plants prefer to grow in evenly moist conditions with little or no drying out between watering. They do not have much water storage other than their fleshy foliage, and the fine root systems are sensitive to drying out.

HUMIDITY
The cool cloud forests that these orchids originally inhabited are full of constant humidity and moderate temperatures. The plants prefer to grow in higher than average humidity conditions, with humidity kept above 60% year-round. Many growers

supplement with frequent misting or growing these plants in terrariums with additional air circulation to satisfy their requirement for cool moist air.

POTTING AND POTTING MIX

Masdevallia orchids need even moisture around their fine root systems and are potted in free-draining fine bark, tree fern, or sphagnum moss mixtures to allow for good drainage around the roots and the moisture retention that they require. The plants are best repotted in the fall, winter, and spring; avoid the hottest months of the year to allow the plants to grow without additional stress caused by repotting. Smaller pots are best to house the compact plants, and potting in too large a container can often lead to problems with the delicate root systems.

FERTILIZER

Masdevallia hybrids are light feeders and can be sensitive to heavy applications of fertilizers. They are best fed every third or fourth watering with a dilute balanced fertilizer solution at one-quarter the recommended strength. Fertilize the plants when they are actively growing, and flush the pots with clear water occasionally to prevent the buildup of fertilizer salts in the medium, which often leads to burned roots and leaf tips.

PESTS AND DISEASES

Masdevallia orchids are relatively pest free and usually only suffer from insect infestations during periods of stress on the plants. Aphids can be a problem with developing flower spikes, buds, and new growth, but with some keen observation and diligence they can be eliminated easily if they are found. Occasionally mealybugs or spider mites can bother the plants in periods of hot weather, but regular grooming and good culture will keep them from getting out of control.

CULTURE NOTES AND TIPS

- *Masdevallia* prefer temperatures below 80–85°F to grow and bloom well. Prolonged periods of high temperatures often result in the plants dropping leaves. Keep them shaded to reduce heat stress on the plants.
- Keep the plants constantly moist and humid to replicate the cloud forest environments of their native habitats.
- Good-quality water is essential and using water with low amounts of dissolved minerals, such as rainwater, is ideal for this group of orchids.

Masdevallia Hybrids
Masd.

Native to Central and South America, with the greatest diversity throughout the Andes, this large genus of miniature species has been popular with orchid collectors for hundreds of years. Many species with the most colorful blooms are found in cool moist habitats in the wild and can dislike high temperatures for prolonged periods, making them a challenge in areas with extended hot humid weather. In recent years, orchid hybridizers have made it a goal to breed plants with brightly colored and patterned blooms with greater warmth tolerance. Look for hybrids created from warmer growing species such as *Masdevallia tonduzii, Masdevallia floribunda*, and *Masdevallia infracta* to get plants that are the most adaptable growers and bloomers. Selections such as *Masdevallia* Copper Angel, *Masdevallia* Ken Dole, *Masdevallia* Peach Fuzz, and *Masdevallia* Sinichi Komoda are warmth-tolerant, compact plants with flowers that are often produced in profusion more than once per year. Masdevallias lack pseudobulbs or other water storage organs, so they need even moisture year-round and higher than average humidity. *Masdevallia* hybrids are excellent choices for moderate to shady conditions, and they grow well alongside *Paphiopedilum* and other miniature species.

The cheerful maroon-speckled blooms of *Masdevallia* Cinnamon Gold are held above the compact foliage.

The white and yellow blooms of *Masdevallia* Mary Staal are produced in profusion on tall wiry stems above the plants in spring.

Maxillaria tenuifolia
Max.

Known for its ease of culture and distinctive fragrance, *Maxillaria tenuifolia* will always be a popular plant. The stacked stems of oval pseudobulbs terminate in a long graceful grass-like leaf, making an attractive tidy mound of foliage over time. The 1-inch chestnut to maroon flowers with a contrasting white spotted lip are borne at the base of the pseudobulbs. Even though the blooms are tucked among the grassy foliage, it is nearly impossible to ignore the strong coconut fragrance that they produce. Native to Mexico and Central America, this species thrives in a wide range of conditions but prefers warmer conditions and bright light.

Even though the flowers can be hidden among the grassy foliage, the powerful fragrance of *Maxillaria tenuifolia* can fill a room.

Maxillaria tenuifolia

Miltoniopsis

Miltoniopsis orchids are prized for their brightly colored and patterned fragrant flowers and have enjoyed increasing interest over the past two decades as breeders have broadened the color range and temperature tolerance of these beautiful orchids. Often called pansy orchids for the strong resemblance of the shape and pattern of the blooms to the common garden pansy (*Viola ×wittrockiana*), the large blooms are also highly fragrant, with a scent often compared to sweet pea or roses. The compact clumping plants are wonderful and rewarding floriferous additions to an orchid collection. About a half dozen naturally occurring species have been used to create an enormous range of large colorful blooms in patterns far beyond what exists in nature.

TEMPERATURE
Day 70–80°F
Night 55–65°F

Native to cool cloud forests in the Andes from Panama and Colombia south to Peru, *Miltoniopsis* species enjoy near constant moisture and moderate cool temperatures. Recent breeding has worked to increase the plants' tolerance for warmer temperatures, as many early hybrids and most of the species do not thrive in areas with warm humid summers. The new hybrids can tolerate short periods with higher temperatures but need to be prevented from drying out and shaded during the warmest months. Especially during periods of warm weather, cooler night temperatures will benefit the plants.

LIGHT
Miltoniopsis are soft thin-leaved plants that appreciate relatively shaded conditions similar to the cloud forests they inhabit in nature. The plants can take some bright light as long as it is filtered and not direct sunlight. If the plants are receiving too much sunlight, the normally soft grayish green foliage will start to develop a rosy pink cast. Light should be monitored closely, especially in the summer or periods of high temperatures, to prevent burning.

WATER
Miltoniopsis orchids don't like to dry out for a long period of time and need constant moisture. The plants should receive frequent regular watering, especially during the warmer months. Good-quality water with low mineral content and dissolved solids is recommended, as hard water can cause leaf tip browning.

HUMIDITY

Miltoniopsis orchids prefer high humidity because of their moisture requirements. Humidity above 50–60% is recommended to help keep the plants from drying out and ward off certain pests and problems.

POTTING AND POTTING MIX

The fine roots of *Miltoniopsis* are intolerant of decomposing potting medium, which is one of the most common sources of failure with this group of orchids. A free-draining and finely textured mix is best. Mixtures with tree fern fiber, fine fir bark, charcoal, and perlite are recommended to ensure proper drainage at all times. The rapid drainage helps to keep the mix aerated and flushes out any accumulated fertilizer salts and sediments. The regular watering required by these orchids encourages the mix to break down more quickly, and thus these orchids should be repotted every 2 years. Keeping the plants slightly pot bound and in shallow pots will help to maintain a happy and healthy root system.

FERTILIZER

Despite their fine roots, *Miltoniopsis* are regular and somewhat heavy feeders. While actively growing, the plants should be fed regularly with a dilute strength balanced fertilizer (20-20-20 or 20-10-20) at one-quarter the recommended strength every second to third watering. As the new growth matures, slightly reduce the frequency and fertilizer concentration.

PESTS AND DISEASES

Common pests to watch for on *Miltoniopsis* include mealybugs, spider mites often associated with low humidity, and thrips and aphids (especially on flowers).

CULTURE NOTES AND TIPS

- *Miltoniopsis* are fine-rooted plants and are intolerant of a mix that has started to break down. They appreciate regular repotting after flowering to help prevent root problems.
- Regular watering is essential for these orchids. The signs of insufficient water appear as wrinkled and distorted foliage and new growth and flowers that do not expand properly.
- Cooler temperatures and humid conditions are preferred for the plants at all times.

Miltoniopsis Hybrids
Mps.

Because they need cool moist conditions without hot weather to thrive, *Miltoniopsis* hybrids were traditionally only grown by specialists. Breeders worked to create plants that had the same colors and patterns of the more challenging hybrids but that are more amenable to cultivation in a wider range of conditions. Although these *Miltoniopsis* hybrids still don't thrive in hot and humid regions of the world, they are certainly easier for the average hobbyist to grow well. All *Miltoniopsis* like cooler conditions and frequent watering, replicating their natural environment in the cloud forests of South America.

TOP The contrasting colors and patterns of *Miltoniopsis* flowers give the plants their common name of pansy orchid.

ABOVE The vibrant colors of *Miltoniopsis* Bert Field show why these hybrids are prized by orchid growers.

Despite a fussy reputation, when *Miltoniopsis* plants are provided with the right conditions they can produce masses of fragrant colorful blooms, like this *Miltoniopsis* Sierra Snows 'Colomborquideas'.

TOP By using the different color forms of species, breeders have begun to create yellow-flowered *Miltoniopsis* hybrids.

ABOVE The flowers of *Miltoniopsis* Martin Orenstein have an intricate design on the lip called a waterfall pattern.

Oncidium &
Oncidium Intergenerics

Commonly called dancing lady orchids because of the brightly patterned and ruffled flowers that resemble colorful costumes of a dancer in motion, this group of South American orchids has been hybridized extensively into a multitude of bright and diverse flower forms. The genus *Oncidium* contains several hundred species and when combined with other related genera such as *Brassia* and *Miltonia* the range of patterns, colors, and flower shapes is virtually endless. Many of these *Oncidium* intergenerics have been widely propagated and, along with *Phalaenopsis*, are among the most popular orchids for the flowering pot plant industry. They are easy to grow and flower, with some of the hybrids blooming more than once per year, making them ideal plants for the beginner.

TEMPERATURE
Day 70–85°F
Night 60–65°F

The genus *Oncidium* is one of the largest and most widespread of all orchid genera in the New World. From tiny miniatures to large epiphytes, the plants are found from the southernmost tip of Florida throughout the Caribbean, Central America, and most of South America. They grow as terrestrials or epiphytes in bright and intermediate to warm tropical forests with year-round moisture.

LIGHT
Oncidium intergenerics enjoy bright filtered light. Situate the plants so they receive several hours of light each day in either an east- or south-facing window. Plants do well under artificial lights and should have some direct light for part of the day, but bright light promotes the best growth and flowering.

WATER
Oncidium orchids like to be kept evenly moist and allowed to dry slightly between watering. The plants produce masses of fine roots, and free-draining mixes with frequent watering suit them best. Not giving enough water can cause distorted new growths with accordion-like pleating on the new foliage.

HUMIDITY

These plants enjoy humidity around 40–60% and are not as humidity sensitive as some other types of orchids. To help increase local humidity around the plants, group them together or place them on shallow pebble-filled trays partially filled with water.

POTTING AND POTTING MIX

Because of their fine root systems, most *Oncidium* intergenerics grow well in a basic fine bark mix with sponge rock and horticultural charcoal. Good drainage is essential for a healthy root system, and plants should be repotted every 1 ½ to 2 years, as they are vigorous growers when happy.

FERTILIZER

For best growth and flowering, the plants should be fed year-round. A balanced fertilizer at one-quarter to one-half the recommended strength every third to fourth watering will help the plants get the best growth and produce the long sprays of flowers—sometimes more than once a year. Fertilizer can be reduced slightly in concentration and frequency during the darker winter months.

PESTS AND DISEASES

Oncidium intergenerics are relatively pest free, and occasional insect infestations can be treated if they are found. Keep watch for aphids on developing flower spikes and buds, and dislodge them with a strong jet of water or a quick spray with a soapy water solution. During periods of hot dry weather, spider mites can become an issue on the thin foliage, but regular syringing of the foliage with water and keeping the humidity up will help to prevent mites from getting out of hand.

CULTURE NOTES AND TIPS

- Keep plants evenly moist and fed throughout the year, as *Oncidium* intergenerics do not have a dormancy period.
- Bright light is best to encourage flowering and produce foliage that is a bright light green.
- Feed plants regularly, and repot frequently to accommodate the vigorous growth and root systems.

Oncidium Intergenerics

The *Oncidium* Alliance includes hundreds of species in a handful of genera, such as *Oncidium, Brassia, Miltonia*, and *Gomesa*, which have been combined by hybridizers in many different directions to produce an extraordinary range of flower sizes, colors, patterns, and numbers. To simplify their extensive and complex pedigree, they are often grouped together under the classification of *Oncidium* Intergenerics, as their culture is relatively the same despite many of the blooms looking radically different from one another. Many familiar orchids are in this group, from the bright golden *Oncidium* Gower Ramsey, a familiar pot plant and cut flower, to the "chocolate orchid" properly called *Oncidium* Sharry Baby. The large purple-spotted starfish-like blooms of *Aliceara* Marfitch 'Howards Dream' and large creamy white flowers of *Aliceara* Tahoma Glacier are borne on long arching inflorescences. *Oncostele* Wildcat has several distinct clones, but all have golden yellow and maroon wildly spotted flowers on tall flower spikes. The plants grow well in bright light, evenly moist conditions, and with fertilizer provided year-round for the vigorous plants. It wouldn't take long to amass a collection of *Oncidium* intergenerics. Even a small collection will provide blooms from early spring through fall, with some plants flowering more than once per year in ideal conditions.

One of the most popular of all orchids, *Oncidium* Sharry Baby 'Sweet Fragrance' has become famous for the powerful, chocolate-like scent of the blooms.

The color forms and patterns of the variable *Oncostele* Wildcat can range from solid mahogany red blooms to yellow and white flowers blotched red and brown.

Like *Odontocidium* Tiger Crow 'Golden Girl', many *Oncidium* intergenerics combine several species and genera to create long-lasting, brightly colored and patterned flowers.

Paphiopedilum

The whimsical and wondrous flowers of *Paphiopedilum* are full of personality and are immediately recognizable. Native to tropical forests in Asia and the Pacific Islands, these orchids live as terrestrials in well-drained soils on the forest floor and on cliffs. Since its early introductions into horticulture, *Paphiopedilum* has been the focus of extensive hybridization that has been used to create a myriad of flower colors and patterns and many with delightful spots, warts, and stripes on the colorful blooms. Many of the available hybrids are easy to cultivate and adaptable subjects perfect for the beginner or advanced hobbyists.

TEMPERATURE
Day 70–80°F
Night 55–65°F

Paphiopedilum species range throughout tropical Asia and south through the Pacific Islands, including Borneo and the Philippines, with most of the species growing as terrestrials in leaf litter and humus on well-drained locations. A few species are known to grow as epiphytes, but they adapt well to cultivation in containers. In nature, the plants grow in intermediate to warm temperatures. Some of the species from the Himalayas and India can tolerate cold temperatures down to 45°F, but most of the mottled-leaf species and other types from the warmer island regions do best at temperatures no lower than 55°F.

LIGHT
Most *Paphiopedilum* orchids prefer medium to low light conditions, as in their natural forest floor habitats. Care must be taken not to give them too much light.

WATER
Paphiopedilum orchids like to be kept moist but not wet. The plants should be allowed to dry slightly between watering but not for long periods. They have large fleshy roots and slightly thickened leaves, but these terrestrial orchids lack the pseudobulbs and water storage ability of many epiphytic orchids.

HUMIDITY

Humidity is not as crucial for *Paphiopedilum* as it is for other orchids. The plants can tolerate lower humidity, with a relative humidity of over 50% suiting them well.

POTTING AND POTTING MIX

Although *Paphiopedilum* orchids are not epiphytes, they rarely grow in soil but instead in layers of decomposing leaf litter and humus. These conditions are easily replicated with a seedling bark mix with added charcoal and perlite for added drainage. The plants benefit from regular repotting and should be repotted every 2 years to keep the mix fresh and free draining.

FERTILIZER

Paphiopedilum orchids are not heavy feeders. They benefit from regular feeding with a balanced fertilizer applied at one-quarter the recommended strength every second or third watering.

PESTS AND DISEASES

Paphiopedilum plants can be prone to mealybug infestations on the foliage and flower spikes, as well as scale occasionally. In conditions with constant low humidity, spider mites can be a problem; these pests should be carefully watched for as they can quickly damage the succulent foliage.

CULTURE NOTES AND TIPS

- *Paphiopedilum* orchids prefer lower light conditions and can easily burn in direct sunlight.
- Regular repotting helps to maintain adequate drainage for the plants.
- Take care when repotting, as the roots can be brittle and are easily broken. Make sure the base of the new growth is in contact with the potting medium to ensure good root initiation and growth.

Paphiopedilum Complex Hybrids

Paph.

Through many generations of selective breeding for larger, rounder, and sometimes spotted or patterned blooms, *Paphiopedilum* complex hybrids have become vastly different from the original group of related species in the pedigree. The large waxy blooms can reach 6 inches or more in diameter. Sometimes maligned as "bulldogs" or "toads" for their large waxy flowers, these orchids are highly prized by collectors willing to pay princely sums for the best forms or flowers. These complex hybrids with long pedigrees were created from a group of closely related species from India, the Himalayas, and China. *Paphiopedilum villosum, Paphiopedilum insigne*, and *Paphiopedilum exul* were bred to create the beautiful colors, patterns, and spots found in these hybrids. The color range includes waxy plum reds, amber, browns and yellows, and green and white flowers with varying numbers of spots. *Paphiopedilum* Hellas, with a beautiful orange amber bloom, *Paphiopedilum* Winston Churchill, with a wine-spotted flower, and *Paphiopedilum* Valerie Tonkin, with a yellow green and white bloom, have been hybridized to create countless beautiful large-flowered progeny. The plants grow under intermediate conditions, with a slightly cooler winter preferred for the best growth and flowering, but they will adapt to warmer conditions as well.

Many complex paphiopedilums, like *Paphiopedilum* Olympic Spots, have earth-toned blooms with contrasting spots and patterns.

Paphiopedilum British Concorde 'Crystelle' is a good example of the long-lasting large waxy blooms of complex paphiopedilums.

Paphiopedilum delenatii
Paph.

Often considered to be among the most beautiful of all *Paphiopedilum* species, this orchid was reportedly first discovered in northern Vietnam in the early 1900s. For many years, all plants in cultivation were descendants of that original handful of plants. In 1990, the species was rediscovered in the wild in southern Vietnam, and a new generation of plants was brought into cultivation, allowing superior and vigorous plants to be bred and shared by slipper orchid enthusiasts. It's easy to see why this species is so popular: its pristine white flower, bright pink pouch, and central yellow staminode make for an elegant combination. *Paphiopedilum delenatii* is a reliable spring bloomer, bearing flowers above the beautifully mottled foliage that makes the plant attractive even out of bloom. It also has the distinction of being one of the few truly fragrant paphiopedilums, with a light rose-like fragrance.

Paphiopedilum delenatii is one of the few sweetly fragrant species of tropical lady's slippers.

Paphiopedilum gratrixianum
Paph.

This orchid is part of a group of closely related species including *Paphiopedilum insigne* and *Paphiopedilum villosum* distributed from India eastward to Vietnam and Laos. *Paphiopedilum gratrixianum* has been an important contributor to many of the modern *Paphiopedilum* complex hybrids. The tall slender stems hold golden amber and white flowers, with a white dorsal sepal blushed pink and centrally spotted purple, high above the foliage. It is an easy species for the beginner, as the plant can tolerate a wide range of temperatures and conditions and is very adaptable to cultivation, making specimens with multiple growths very quickly.

Paphiopedilum gratrixianum is one of the most floriferous lady's slipper species.

Paphiopedilum Greyi
Paph.

The Bracypetalum section of *Paphiopedilum* is native to Southeast Asia. The plants are relatively small and have dark green patterned leaves and cream to white flowers with dark chestnut spots, speckles, or lines. These species grow on well-drained, often dry limestone cliffs in their native habitats. They can be a little challenging for the beginning orchid grower because they prefer slightly drier and brighter conditions than species native to shaded wet tropical forests. *Paphiopedilum* Greyi is a primary hybrid between *Paphiopedilum godefroyae* and *Paphiopedilum niveum* that has gained all the delicate grace and pattern of the parents with the addition of hybrid vigor. The plants prefer to be pot bound, and the medium should not be allowed to become saturated.

Paphiopedilum Julius
Paph.

This multifloral paphiopedilum is a hybrid between the colorful *Paphiopedilum lowii* and *Paphiopedilum rothschildianum* with all the finest attributes of its parents. It produces large light green spotted and striped blooms with long horizontal mustache-like magenta pink petals. The individual blooms can easily be 8 inches across, and the foliage can span 24 inches across from tip to tip. The large growing plants can take several years to reach maturity from seed but the spectacular multifloral inflorescence is well worth the wait. If you can provide the space, warmer and brighter conditions, and patience, *Paphiopedilum* Julius is an impressive and prized plant for any orchid collection.

The large stately blooms of *Paphiopedilum* Julius are quite impressive.

Paphiopedilum Lynleigh Koopowitz
Paph.

In the late 1980s, a group of related species were discovered in the mountains of China and later in Vietnam. These orchids with fantastic and colorful flowers, although desirable, proved to be challenging to grow even by experienced orchid enthusiasts. Intrepid orchid breeders began making hybrids between the more challenging species and the vigorous *Paphiopedilum delenatii*. The resulting plants had all the color and pattern in foliage and flower as the wild species but with increased vigor and ease of cultivation. *Paphiopedilum* Lynleigh Koopowitz has proven to be a standout among these hybrids. It produces stately colorful blooms borne on tall stems over velvety reticulated foliage. To flower well, this group of species and hybrids seems to appreciate a slightly cooler and drier winter. Some growers report that by doing this it helps the plants bloom more regularly.

The tall flower spikes and fanciful blooms of *Paphiopedilum* Lynleigh Koopowitz are prized by orchid collectors.

Paphiopedilum Maudiae Hybrids
Paph.

The original hybrid *Paphiopedilum* Maudiae was created more than a century ago and became the foundation for many generations of hybrids. Maudiae hybrids are also referred to as mottled-leaved paphiopedilums for their checkered and patterned foliage. The single or uncommonly double blooms are borne on tall stems above attractive foliage. The addition of new color forms and species has increased the color range available, provided new patterns and spots, and expanded the overall diversity of this popular group of orchids. They are some of the best orchids for the beginner in any climate or situation and perform well in lower light or slightly shaded conditions.

Paphiopedilum Maudiae helped to spawn a new direction in orchid hybrids.

By hybridizing closely related species, breeders have increased the range of colors and patterns in tropical lady's slipper orchids. *Paphiopedilum* Raingreen's Legend is the result of crossing seven *Paphiopedilum* species.

Orchid breeders have continued selecting for well-defined markings, color contrast, and deep color saturation, as seen in *Paphiopedilum* Bob Nagel 'New Horizon'.

Paphiopedilum Pinocchio
Paph.

Most *Paphiopedilum* species produce a single flower at the end of the tall stem. A few of the species can produce single blooms successively over a period of several months, and this deservedly popular hybrid is one of them. *Paphiopedilum* Pinocchio can be in bloom continuously for a year or more, producing whimsical spotted pastel blooms. It is an easy and forgiving plant for the beginner and experienced orchidists alike.

Paphiopedilum Saint Swithin
Paph.

Paphiopedilum rothschildianum, native to Borneo, is sometimes referred to as the King of Orchids because of its regal tall stems of large striped flowers. The plants can take many years to reach blooming size and, as a result, often command a kingly price. *Paphiopedilum* Saint Swithin is a hybrid produced by crossing *Paph. rothschildianum* with the related *Paphiopedilum philippinense*. It is a vigorous plant with large strap-leaved foliage. Up to six or seven contrasting stripped flowers with mustache-like petals reaching over 8 inches from tip to tip are borne on stems that can stand 36 inches tall. For best growth and flowering, many of the larger multifloral or strap-leaved paphiopedilums appreciate warmer conditions year-round and slightly brighter light than other plants in the genus.

Paphiopedilum Saint Swithin bears three to six flowers per stem, making an elegant and bold statement.

Paphiopedilum spicerianum
Paph.

This native of India, Bhutan, and southern China is found in moist and shaded places among pockets of leaf litter on limestone cliffs. It was discovered and introduced into cultivation more than a century ago. Since then it has been used extensively in breeding and is in the pedigree of many *Paphiopedilum* hybrids. *Paphiopedilum spicerianum* is a reliable fall-blooming species; it has green and purple flowers with a contrasting bright white dorsal sepal borne just above a compact plant. It is an easy plant to cultivate and can quickly fill out a 4-inch pot, making delightful specimens in a small amount of space.

Paphiopedilum spicerianum is a reliable fall-blooming compact plant.

Phaius

Medium to large plants with palm-like leaves, *Phaius* orchids make excellent subjects for the tropical landscape or home with space for the broad leaves and tall spikes of flowers. The plants produce colorful blooms in spring to early summer and are easy to grow and tolerant of a wide range of conditions. These terrestrial orchids deserve wider cultivation as they are rewarding and easy subjects for the beginner or expert orchid enthusiast.

TEMPERATURE
Day 65–85°F
Night 55–65°F

Native to Asia and the Pacific Islands, these medium to large terrestrial orchids are commonly found in moist habitats with bright light. Plants experience temperatures ranging from 50 to 85°F in the wild. Colder temperatures might damage foliage, but the plants will usually survive and regrow from the pseudobulbs.

LIGHT
Phaius orchids prefer medium to bright light, despite the delicate look of the foliage. The plants grow best in strong light conditions; when healthy, the foliage should be a bright light green, not dark or olive green. Plants will flower under low light, but failure to bloom is often due to low light conditions.

WATER
When in active growth, *Phaius* orchids require constant moisture. Some of the more common species are found growing in swamps or other areas with lots of moisture around the roots of the plants. Plants can be kept slightly drier when the growths are mature in fall to early winter.

HUMIDITY
Phaius orchids require moderate amounts of humidity and are best kept in conditions with an average humidity above 50%. The foliage of plants exposed to warm dry air for long periods often develops brown edges and tips, and these conditions encourage certain types of pests, such as spider mites.

POTTING AND POTTING MIX
Phaius orchids are terrestrial plants and grow best in mixes with fine bark, charcoal, and perlite to support their vigorous root systems. The plants aren't too particular about the potting mix, as long as it holds moisture, and will even grow in soilless

mixes (ProMix) or sphagnum moss. They are best repotted shortly after blooming as the new growth starts to develop.

FERTILIZER

Phaius plants are heavy feeders when in active growth and appreciate applications of full-strength balanced fertilizers on a regular basis. Fertilizers can be applied with every other watering, and some growers use slow-release fertilizers (such as Osmocote or Nutricote) around the roots. During the fall and winter, fertilizer applications can be reduced to one-half to one-quarter the concentration.

PESTS AND DISEASES

The thin foliage of *Phaius* orchids is attractive to piercing and sucking insects, and regular inspections should be done to make sure there are no appearances of scale, mealybugs, thrips, or spider mites. The plants appreciate regular syringing of the foliage with water to help them grow, increase humidity, and prevent insect infestations.

CULTURE NOTES AND TIPS

- *Phaius* orchids bloom best in bright light conditions.
- The plants are heavy feeders and need regular applications of fertilizer when they are actively growing.
- These terrestrial orchids appreciate even constant moisture during the growing season.
- The vigorous root systems need room to grow. Repot these plants after flowering in fresh soil on an annual basis.

Phaius Hybrids

Phaius hybrids are large terrestrial orchids often grown as landscape plants in tropical climates because of their ease of culture and vigor. The large pleated foliage and imposing flower spikes can easily reach 5 feet tall when happy, producing many flowers per inflorescence and putting on an impressive display when grown well. Despite their need for space and unusual appearance, they are easy to grow as long as they receive sufficient moisture and food for the large plants. The large root systems prefer a potting medium with some peat mixture added. The thin leaves of *Phaius* hybrids can be prone to attack by spider mites and scale, so keep watch for hidden pests to make sure infestations do not get out of hand.

TOP *Phaius* hybrids, like *Phaius* Microburst 'Orchtoberfest', are easy to grow indoors if you have space for the large plants.

RIGHT *Phaius tankervillae* makes a beautiful addition to the garden in tropical climates.

Phalaenopsis

Without question, the most popular and widely cultivated orchids in the world are *Phalaenopsis*. This genus of orchids has been the leader in the renaissance of home orchid growing over the past decade. They are an easy and adaptable group of orchids with an incredible range of flower colors and patterns and plant sizes. They are among the easiest orchids to grow and bloom in the home, and in the right conditions the long-lasting blooms can reward you with flowers for several months.

TEMPERATURE
Day 65–85°F
Night 55–60°F

The nearly 60 species in this genus are mostly medium to small epiphytic plants distributed from India and China to Thailand, Borneo, Sumatra, Indonesia, and the Philippines. In their native habitats, most *Phalaenopsis* species grow in warm humid lowland forests with even temperatures and moisture throughout the year. Many of the species never experience temperatures much below 50°F in the wild, and these orchids are best grown in warmer conditions away from cold of any kind.

LIGHT
Phalaenopsis orchids require less light than most other orchids to grow and bloom. The plants can tolerate bright light as long as it is filtered through a sheer curtain, as the leaves can burn easily in high light conditions. They also perform well under artificial light conditions.

WATER
Phalaenopsis plants do not have any water storage organs other than their fleshy leaves, so they need to be kept evenly moist without any major drying out. The plants should only be allowed to approach dryness before watering again. Watering might be done more frequently in hot weather and more sparingly in cool weather, depending on the potting medium. Plants grown in moss will dry more slowly than those grown in a bark mix. *Phalaenopsis* plants are commonly infected with crown rot if water is allowed to sit in the terminal growth. If water happens to get in the crown when watering, gently remove it with a paper towel to avoid problems later.

HUMIDITY
Although *Phalaenopsis* orchids can tolerate lower than average humidity, they do prefer to grow where the humidity is above 65%. You can increase the humidity around plants by growing them on pebble-filled trays partially filled with water, or cluster plants together to create a microclimate of higher humidity.

POTTING AND POTTING MIX

Phalaenopsis plants grow well in a mix suited for epiphytic orchids. A basic bark mixture with some added perlite and charcoal for drainage suits them well and allows the proper balance of air and moisture around the roots. *Phalaenopsis* orchids are commonly produced in densely packed pots of sphagnum moss, and plants grow well in the moss. This type of potting usually dries slowly, but care must be taken to avoid the moss becoming soggy for long periods of time.

FERTILIZER

Phalaenopsis orchids grow best with regular feeding of balance fertilizer at one-half the recommended strength. To get the best growth and flowering, feed plants year-round with fertilizer applied every second or third watering during the warmest months, when growth is fastest. Fertilizer can be reduced slightly but not completely during the cooler months, because the plants do not go dormant.

PESTS AND DISEASES

Watch for mealybugs and aphids on developing flower spikes and at the backs of the blooms, where they like to hide. Scale and mites can occasionally be a problem on *Phalaenopsis*, especially on weakened or dehydrated plants. Most small infestations can easily be dispatched with a strong jet of water or soapy water solutions, and pesticides might only be necessary in the event of large or persistent infestation. One of the more common disease problems with *Phalaenopsis* is bacterial rot caused by water sitting in the new growth. Careful watering and making sure the plants are dry before nightfall is the best way to control crown rot in *Phalaenopsis*.

CULTURE NOTES AND TIPS

- *Phalaenopsis* orchids are warm-growing plants and do best with temperatures over 60°F year-round. Avoid cold drafts, which can lead to buds dropping off prematurely.
- They are lower light orchids and care must be taken to not burn the foliage. Plants are best grown in bright diffuse light, such as set back slightly from an east- or south-facing window to avoid direct sunlight.
- Because they grow year-round, the plants require regular feeding and watering. Do not allow them to go completely dry for long periods.
- Keep water out of the crown and make sure that the plants are dry before nightfall to avoid disease.
- After flowering, remove the bloom spike entirely. This allows the plant to recover and grow new roots and leaves to store up energy for next year's blooms.

Phalaenopsis Baldan's Kaleidoscope 'Golden Treasure'
Phal.

This hybrid's unusual golden yellow flowers with a heavy overlay of scarlet red veins create a striking combination reminiscent of a glowing sunset. Many mericlones were produced from the original plant, and it is now considered a benchmark variety for modern *Phalaenopsis* hybrids. It is a vigorous hybrid and over time makes wonderful specimens with multiple branched flower spikes and many long-lasting blooms. Easy and floriferous, this plant is an excellent choice for the beginning orchid grower looking for something a little different than your typical white *Phalaenopsis*.

Phalaenopsis Baldan's Kaleidoscope has remained popular for the beautifully patterned flowers and floriferous nature.

Phalaenopsis bellina
Phal.

Within *Phalaenopsis*, several species are prized by orchid collectors because they possess a beauty and grace that is different than the large blooms of the modern hybrids. One of the most popular is *Phalaenopsis bellina*, native to Malaysia and Borneo, with chartreuse green and magenta blooms on short flower spikes that rest just above the glossy fans of bright green leaves. The flowers are produced in late spring to early summer and have a delightful fragrance with notes of spice and citrus, making the plant a favorite of hobbyists and fragrance enthusiasts alike. On mature plants, the spikes will continue to branch and produce more flowers over many years as long as they remain green. The plants grow well in low light conditions and warm temperatures, and they do well under artificial lights.

Phalaenopsis bellina is a warm-growing orchid prized for the intense sweet fragrance from flowers that can bloom continuously for months.

Phalaenopsis Hybrids
Phal.

Phalaenopsis hybrids provide a full color range of yellow, orange, spots, stripes, and wildly spotted and patterned flowers that continue to delight collectors and hobbyists the world over. They are forgiving, easy, long-blooming plants and are among the best orchids for the beginning home orchid grower. Hybridizers have started to look in several different directions, including true miniatures that flower when under 6 inches tall, breeding fragrant species back into modern hybrids to impart fragrance, and even breeding for colored and patterned foliage. A popular group at the moment is miniature multifloral *Phalaenopsis*. They produce many smaller flowers on branched inflorescences over compact plants. Some are miniaturized versions of larger varieties, whereas others have completely new flower forms, patterns, and fragrances not seen before in standard varieties. These hybrids also tend to produce multiple fans of leaves that eventually make a compact clump of foliage with multiple flower spikes all blooming at once. *Phalaenopsis* miniature multiflorals are just as easy to grow and as floriferous as their larger cousins in a fraction of the space. Harlequin *Phalaenopsis* have flowers that look blotched and painted with color, and all are descended from one unusual plant that was discovered by a breeder. Another recent trend is breeding *Phalaenopsis* with wide open lips rather than the rolled edges found on a typical bloom, which makes the flowers look larger and rounder compared to normal *Phalaenopsis* blooms.

TOP Breeders have worked to create compact plants with long-lasting branching flower spikes, including *Phalaenopsis*. Brother Orange Runabout

ABOVE RIGHT *Phalaenopsis* Taisuco Swan produces pristine long-lasting blooms.

RIGHT The saturated orange of *Phalaenopsis* Surf Song blooms is just one of the huge range of colors created by *Phalaenopsis* breeders.

Phalaenopsis schilleriana
Phal.

One of the most beautiful of orchid species in or out of bloom, this Philippine native is still as popular with orchid collectors as it was when it was first introduced into cultivation over 150 years ago. In the breeding of modern *Phalaenopsis*, this species is used for the delicate branched inflorescences with light pink and yellow flowers that on a mature specimen look like a cloud of butterflies in flight. The softly fragrant flowers smell sweetly of roses and are produced in profusion from this vigorous compact plant. The foliage is dark green and covered with silver spots and bars, adding to the plant's interest and beauty out of flower.

Phalaenopsis schilleriana has exquisite leaves patterned with silver spots and branching cascades of fragrant pink blooms.

Phalaenopsis Sogo Yukidian
Phal.

Hundreds of standard white *Phalaenopsis* hybrids have been produced since the early 1940s, after the introduction of *Phalaenopsis* Doris, the plant considered to be the first modern white. Breeders are continually selecting for larger and rounder flowers, overlapping segments, size, and vigor. The hybrid *Phalaenopsis* Sogo Yukidian is one of the finest standard white *Phalaenopsis* introduced by orchid breeders. The enormous white blooms can reach over 6 inches in diameter, and large healthy specimen plants can easily produce a flower spike with more than 20 blooms, creating quite an impressive sight.

Phragmipedium

The American tropical lady's slipper orchids are found from Central America south throughout the Andes and into Brazil. They are semi-terrestrial orchids found in moist habitats with heavy rainfall and moderate temperatures. The slipper flowers strongly resemble their Asian counterparts in the genus *Paphiopedilum*. Many have long narrow twisted petals that hang from the flower like ribbons, and some species have petals that can dangle nearly a meter long. Other plants in the genus have brightly colored orange, pink, or even red blooms in unusual colors for slipper orchids. *Phragmipedium* orchids often produce successive flowers on a single stem over several months in spring and early summer. They are vigorous, trouble-free plants in the right conditions and are worthwhile additions to any orchid collection.

TEMPERATURE
Day 70–80°F
Night 55–65°F

Phragmipedium species are native to Central and South America. Because they grow on steep embankments and slopes, the plants are exposed to bright light to full sun for most of the day. They grow in intermediate to warm conditions year-round, with little or no seasonal change in temperature.

LIGHT
Unlike many other slipper orchids, *Phragmipedium* plants prefer good amounts of sunlight to grow and bloom their best. Plants should be positioned in bright filtered light with shade provided, especially in the hottest periods of the year, to prevent the thin leaves from burning. The foliage should be bright green, indicating the plants are getting enough sunlight.

WATER
Phragmipedium orchids like regular heavy watering to grow and bloom well. If conditions are too dry, the leaf tips often burn and turn brown. In nature, many species are found in areas with frequent rainfall and enjoy similar conditions when grown in the home. These orchids can tolerate sitting in a saucer of water to help provide the amount of moisture they need, and phragmipediums are the perfect plant for the person who has a tendency to overwater.

HUMIDITY

These tropical slipper orchids are from moist environments, and they prefer relative humidity of 60–80%. However, they can tolerate slightly lower humidity as long as they are watered properly.

POTTING AND POTTING MIX

Although *Phragmipedium* plants prefer lots of moisture, good drainage is essential for a healthy root system. The plants do well in fine bark mixes with added perlite and charcoal. They produce strong root systems and should have a pot that allows for vigorous root growth. Taller pots are preferable to shallow ones because they provide better drainage.

FERTILIZER

Phragmipedium orchids should be fed regularly throughout the year. Provide a balanced fertilizer (20-20-20) at one-quarter strength every third to fourth watering.

PESTS AND DISEASES

Phragmipedium plants are relatively pest free when they are healthy and strong. Keep watch for occasional mealybugs or aphids on the flower stems and buds. Groom and remove dead foliage when repotting, as this can provide hiding places for mealybugs and scale insects.

CULTURE NOTES AND TIPS

- *Phragmipedium* orchids need abundant and regular watering to grow well.
- These orchids appreciate repotting every 1 to 2 years. Sink the plants slightly lower in the pot to accommodate the slightly climbing growth habit.
- Bright filtered light encourages the best flowering.

Phragmipedium Don Wimber
Phrag.

In the early 1980s, *Phragmipedium besseae* was discovered in Peru. The species' unique scarlet orange blooms generated great excitement among hybridizers, who saw the new potential color range to be explored through selective breeding. *Phragmipedium* Don Wimber is a fine example of their efforts. The plant can produce many glowing peach blooms in succession on tall branched stems. The slightly climbing habit of the plants requires some finesse in repotting, but the extra efforts will be rewarded with impressive specimens in a relatively short period of time.

Phragmipedium Don Wimber can bloom for many months, producing successive apricot orange flowers on tall stems.

Phragmipedium Grande
Phrag.

This hybrid produces stately 24- to 36-inch-tall flower spikes borne above strong clumping plants that multiply rapidly. The green and brown flowers of *Phragmipedium* Grande, with long hanging ribbon-like petals, are produced in succession. When several flowers are open, it makes for a dramatic presentation. Like many phragmipediums, this plant enjoys regular and liberal applications of water during the year, with regular dilute feedings to allow the plants to reach their maximum potential.

The petals of *Phragmipedium* Grande hang like twisted ribbons from the flowers.

Phragmipedium Memoria Dick Clements
Phrag.

The cross between the scarlet-flowered *Phragmipedium besseae* and the green and maroon *Phragmipedium sargentianum* has produced many excellent progeny, which, like *Phragmipedium* Memoria Dick Clements, have dark red flowers with excellent shape and color. Younger plants produce single blooms in succession, but as plants get older they can hold multiple flowers on a branching stem, making for a striking display. The plants are worth every effort and the time needed to cultivate them for the long term.

Phragmipedium Sedenii
Phrag.

This classic *Phragmipedium* hybrid, a favorite of orchid collectors for many years, is known for vigorous growth and flowering and easy care. It is more compact than some *Phragmipedium* hybrids and has delicate pink and white speckled flowers borne successively over several months in spring to early summer. Larger specimens can bloom continuously for long periods. The plants are relatively pest free and enjoy regular watering and dilute feeding. When happy, they produce extensive root systems that benefit from regular repotting.

Pleurothallids

The term pleurothallids is used by orchid enthusiasts when referring to the Pleurothallidinae, a big name for a group of mostly miniature orchids. Although many of the names of these plants have recently changed, they are all closely related and enjoy similar conditions. The pleurothallids are mostly miniature species from Central and South America prized for their diversity in form and flower, compact size, and floriferous nature. This group contains larger and colorful plants such as *Masdevallia* orchids but the smaller, more curious, insect-like blooms of plants such as *Stelis* and *Specklinia* should not be overlooked as they are extremely rewarding plants to add to a mixed orchid collection. Some of the species can be large bulky plants, but the miniatures *Specklinia grobyi* (syn. *Pleurothallis grobyi*), *Stelis ornata* (syn. *Pleurothallis ornata*), and *Specklinia tribuloides* (syn. *Pleurothallis tribuloides*) make attractive tufted plants that flower profusely in intermediate to warm conditions. You might need a magnifying glass to appreciate the minute details of the flowers, but they are full of color and personality. *Specklinia grobyi* produces a cloud of pale yellow blooms hovering above the foliage. In the tiny blooms of *Stelis ornata*, each sepal is adorned with white tassels that move at the slightest breeze. *Specklinia tribuloides* has appropriately been called the lobster orchid because its rust orange flowers look like lobster claws hidden among the foliage. These species orchids prefer even moisture throughout the year, and they should only be allowed to dry slightly between watering. These miniature plants are best grown mounted or in small pots, where the delightful foliage and flowers can be easily appreciated up close.

The diminutive plants of *Speklinia grobyi* (syn. *Pleurothallis grobyi*) produce spikes of tiny flowers that appear to hover above the tufts of rounded foliage.

TOP The strange bird beak flowers of *Pleurothallis nossax* are produced in succession from the center of the leaf.

ABOVE RIGHT The curious small maroon flowers of *Acianthera pubescens* (syn. *Pleurothallis pubescens*) are produced in abundance from the foliage.

RIGHT *Pleurothallis truncata* produces charming chains of tiny orange blooms across the surface of the leaves.

Prosthechea cochleate
syn. *Encyclia cochleata*
Psh.

Sometimes referred to as the cockleshell orchid or octopus orchid, this widespread species is found from southern Florida through Central America and northern South America. Unlike many orchid species, the dark purple lip is uppermost on the flower, with the twisted chartreuse yellow sepals and petals hanging downward like the tentacles of a sea creature. The flowers are produced in succession over a long period in late spring through summer, and mature plants can produce these delightful flowers for several months. *Prosthechea cochleata* is an easy and durable species that prefers medium to bright light and intermediate to warm conditions and makes an unusual addition to any orchid collection.

Appropriately named the octopus orchid, *Prosthechea cochleata* can bloom continually for several months.

Psychopsis Kahili
Pyp.

This hybrid between several of the famed butterfly orchid species that fueled the Victorian orchid craze is much easier to grow than the wild species. The broad leathery leaves are lightly mottled and sit well below the tall wiry inflorescences tipped with the outrageous blooms of orange and yellow, which bear an uncanny resemblance to a tropical butterfly in flight. The inflorescence can produce successive blooms for many years, so don't cut the flower spike as long as it is still green. These unusual orchids prefer bright light, growing on the dry side, and no strong disturbance of the roots. They are also very prone to rot when the new growth is developing, so take extra care when watering during this period of growth.

The incredible blooms of the butterfly orchid sparked the trend in growing and collecting orchids after the plant was introduced to European gardens.

Renanthera Kalsom 'Red Dragon'

Ren.

It's hard to imagine an orchid flower that has a brighter red color than those of *Renanthera* hybrids. Although not the easiest plants to grow in the home, they are certainly desirable for those with the ability and space to grow these lanky beauties. The narrow tall stems of *Renanthera* Kalsom 'Red Dragon' are covered with alternating leaves and require support, as they can get quite tall over time—eventually over 6 feet tall in the best environments. The monopodial stems produce surprisingly large, nearly horizontal branching inflorescences with dozens of 2-inch glowing cherry red blooms along the stem that look like a swarm of butterflies in flight. Like other vandaceous plants, *Renanthera* orchids require warm conditions, with temperatures above 65°F year-round, bright light, and high humidity to perform well.

The cascades of bright red flowers of *Renanthera* Kalsom are worth the extra effort that it takes to grow these plants outside of the warm tropical environments they thrive in.

Rhyncattleanthe Burana Beauty

syn. *Potinara* Burana Beauty

Rth.

Over the past couple of decades, there has been an increase in *Cattleya* breeding in Thailand, and some of the resulting hybrids have been quite spectacular. One of the more successful of these new hybrids is *Rhyncattleyanthe* Burana Beauty. The shocking bicolored chrome yellow and red splashed flowers are produced in clusters just above the compact upright growth. The plants are extremely vigorous and grow in many directions, making specimens with abundant clusters of the brightly patterned blooms. The added bonus is the strong citrus fragrance that the flowers produce during the day, filling any space with their perfume. The blooms can be produced more than once a year. This hybrid grows easily in typical *Cattleya* conditions with bright filtered light and intermediate to warm temperatures.

Rhyncattleanthe Dan O'Neil 'Jubilee'

syn. *Brassolaeliocattleya* Dan O'Neil 'Jubilee'
Rth.

Compact *Cattleya* hybrids are enjoying a surge in popularity, with many breeders concentrating on producing smaller plants with long-lasting colorful blooms. Some of the standard *Cattleya* can be quite large, but these newer compact hybrids are excellent choices for a *Cattleya* lover with limited space. *Rhyncattleanthe* Dan O'Neil 'Jubilee' is an excellent choice, with firm long-lasting flowers. The glowing orange blooms with a delicate red picotee are hard to ignore. The plant is a strong grower and reliable spring bloomer under medium to bright light and intermediate to warm conditions.

The waxy orange blooms of *Rhynattleanthe* Dan O'Neil 'Jubilee' are long lasting and produced on compact plants.

Rhyncholaelia digbyana

Rl.

Orchid hybridizers continue to turn to this species to add substance and to capture that elusive bright green color of the blooms of this species in their creations. This species is an important contributing ancestor of most modern *Cattleya* hybrids, transforming the fringe of the natural species into the undulating and ruffled edge of the lip so characteristic of these hybrids, and its name is included in the hybrid genus *Rhyncholaeliocattleya*. Native to dry forests from Mexico south through much of Central America, this *Cattleya* relative is famous for its large waxy blooms with a heavily fringed lip. The 4- to 5-inch blooms are borne in summer and have an intense citrus and lemon scent, especially after dark, perfuming the surrounding air. Coming from dry areas where the plants grow in bright light, this species prefers being grown a little brighter and drier than most *Cattleya* orchids.

The fringed citrus-scented blooms of *Rhyncholaelia digbyana* are produced in early summer.

Rhyncholaeliocattleya Burdekin Wonder
syn. *Brassolaeliocattleya* Burdekin Wonder
Rlc.

The large, fragrant, ruffled blooms of classic white *Cattleya* orchids have always been popular. Although it would be difficult to choose just one of these, *Rhyncholaeliocattleya* Burdekin Wonder is a consistent performer that's readily available. The large ruffled, fragrant, clear white flowers are offset with a yellow green disk on the center of the lip and are wonderfully fragrant. The individual blooms can be nearly 7 inches in diameter on compact plants that grow 12 to 18 inches tall. When well established and growing, it's not unusual for this spring bloomer to produce an additional flush of showy blooms again in the fall.

The classic white-and-yellow blooms of *Rhyncholaelio-cattleya* Burdekin Wonder are still popular today.

Rhyncholaeliocattleya George King 'Serendipity'
syn. *Brassolaeliocattleya* George King 'Serendipity'
Rlc.

For over 100 years *Cattleya* hybridizers have been breeding plants hoping to improve the form, fragrance, and color range. In the late 1960s and 1970s, hybridizers worked toward creating flowers in warm tones, often referred to as "art shades" for their layered and mixed-tone blooms of apricots, blush yellows, and soft oranges. *Rhyncholaeliocattleya* George King 'Serendipity' was selected for the unique light pink flowers that age into salmon orange. The highly fragrant blooms are produced in late winter on a vigorous compact plant that is deservedly still popular in collections 40 years after its introduction.

The peach-colored blooms of *Rhyncolaeliocattleya* George King 'Serendipity' are sought out by collectors for their unique color.

Rhyncholaeliocattleya
Goldenzelle 'Lemon Chiffon'
syn. *Brassolaeliocattleya* Goldenzelle 'Lemon Chiffon'
Rlc.

Considered by many *Cattleya* breeders to be one of the greatest of all time, *Rhyncholaeliocattleya* Goldenzelle was bred by the historically famous Stewart Orchids of Carpinteria, California. A few clones were selected from the original cross and 'Lemon Chiffon' is one of the best. The plant is a reliable and prolific bloomer, and the clear lemon yellow flowers with a contrasting red splash on the lip never fail to attract attention. The strong upright stems present the highly fragrant flowers nicely, allowing them to show well without additional staking or support.

Rhyncholaeliocattleya Goldenzelle 'Lemon Chiffon' is considered by many collectors to be a benchmark in *Cattleya* hybridizing.

Rhyncholaeliocattleya
Malworth 'Orchidglade'
syn. *Brassolaeliocattleya* Malworth 'Orchidglade'
Rlc.

For many years, orchid enthusiasts and breeders have debated the true pedigree of this hybrid. The one thing that most can agree on is that the plant is a benchmark in yellow *Cattleya* breeding. Bred by the historically famous Jones & Scully Orchidglade in Florida, it still holds the test of time. This vigorous and floriferous hybrid produces several large blooms atop the upright foliage during late winter. The golden yellow blooms with a slight pink flush are heavily perfumed with a sweet lem-

The large yellow orange blooms of *Rhyncholaeiiocattleya* Malworth 'Orchidglade' are long lasting and strongly fragrant of lemon and citrus.

ony fragrance that is absolutely delightful. The plant is a vigorous grower, forming multiple leads and making specimens in short time. The individual pseudobulbs are more than 18 inches tall, making the plant a little robust for some collections, but it's well worth making the space for the superb combination of color and fragrance of these blooms.

Rhynchostylis gigantea
Rhy.

This widely distributed species is found from India east toward Thailand, Vietnam, and China and south through Borneo and the Philippines. *Rhynchostylis gigantea* produces long foxtail inflorescences of brightly colored waxy blooms that are powerfully fragrant during the day. Despite the relatively small size of the blooms, their incense-like perfume fills the air around the plants. *Rhynchostylis* plants produce thick coarse root systems on slow-growing monopodial plants with ridged foliage. The plants have been selectively bred to introduce different color forms beyond the white flowers spotted pink, and now deep red, orange, magenta blotched, and even pure white forms have become popular in horticulture. The plants grow and flower best in an open mix with warm temperatures and a slightly shaded location.

The colorful fragrant blooms of *Rhynchostylis gigantea* make them popular plants for warm humid climates.

Spiranthes speciosa
Spir.

Many terrestrial orchids have a reputation for being difficult to grow, needing very exacting soil and culture conditions to thrive. This Central American species defies that reputation. Growing very well alongside paphiopedilums and other lower light plants, *Spiranthes speciosa* produces bright red leaf-like bracts along the flower stem and the tubular blooms emerge from within. At first glance, the plant might look more like a bromeliad, but closer examination reveals the characteristic orchid blooms. The rosettes of soft green foliage sprout from large fleshy roots, making specimens in a short period. The plants benefit from the addition of peat moss or a soilless potting mix to their medium. Don't be discouraged if some of the foliage dies back after flowering, as the plants will produce new foliage with the flush of growth in spring to summer.

Tolumnia

Formerly called Equitant *Oncidium*, these compact brightly colored orchids make wonderful additions to any windowsill or greenhouse collection. The plants are native to the Caribbean, where they often grow in exposed locations on twigs and small branches, producing brightly colored flowers on wiry stems. Orchid breeders have created a swarm of hybrids using many of the species, and the flowers are now available in a veritable carnival of colors and patterns. *Tolumnia* plants can be a challenge for some to grow, but their culture requirements can be mastered with a little practice.

TEMPERATURE
Day 70–85°F
Night 65–70°F

Native to the Caribbean, the plants rarely experience cold conditions in the wild and are best cultivated at temperatures above 65°F. If the plants are exposed to cold temperatures, keep them on the dry side, as they can quickly rot if they are cold and wet.

LIGHT
These orchids prefer bright light conditions. It's completely normal for the plants to develop purple or reddish coloring on their foliage in response to strong light. Many *Tolumnia* species and hybrids only flower well when exposed to bright light conditions, and lack of sunlight is often the cause for shy blooming.

WATER
The plants require frequent watering or heaving misting, but also should be allowed to dry out between watering. This mimics their native environment, where they receive water from regular rain or fog but then dry out from buoyant air movement. Overwatering the plants is a common cause of failure with *Tolumnia*, and it's best to heavily mist the plants in the morning, which allows them to dry by nightfall.

HUMIDITY
The plants are from areas with relatively high natural humidity and need a relative humidity of 50% when grown in cultivation. Regular misting can help to increase the humidity, but the plants should be allowed to dry by nightfall.

POTTING AND POTTING MIX

Tolumnia orchids are found in nature with their roots exposed and prefer to have an open well-drained mix for their fine roots. The plants do well mounted, in small baskets, or in terra cotta pots with very little potting medium around their roots. Mixes that retain too much moisture often result in quick rotting of the roots and a resulting decline in the plants. It is surprising how well these orchids do with just a few pieces of charcoal or bark to support the plants in their small pots.

FERTILIZER

These small plants appreciate regular feeding with dilute fertilizer at one-quarter the recommended strength. A balanced fertilizer works well, and they respond with quick growth and blooming when fed and watered well.

PESTS AND DISEASES

Tolumnia orchids are relatively pest free but still can become infested by mealybugs and scale insects, which like to hide in the small tight fans of foliage. Aphids are a common pest of the developing flower spikes but are easily controlled. Thrips and spider mite can become an issue in warmer months, but they rarely seem to bother the plants.

CULTURE NOTES AND TIPS

- Allow the plants to dry between watering, and ensure they don't remain too wet especially around the roots.
- Do not pot the plants in too large of a container. Grow them in small pots or baskets to allow good air circulation around the roots, which helps them to dry out freely and mimics their natural growing environment.
- Watering can be done through regular misting of the plants. Allow them to dry before nightfall.

Tolumnia Hybrids
Tolu.

From a small original group of closely related species native to the Caribbean, orchid hybridizers have created many *Tolumnia* hybrids with colorful blooms held above small 4- to 6-inch fans of foliage. The compact plants are native to dry sunny environments, where they grow on small twigs with their roots exposed to light rains and good air movement. In cultivation, they thrive in small pots in bright locations where they can be easily watered by a good heavy misting every couple of days. They are trouble-free plants, as long as they get the sunlight they need, and will reward your efforts with bright flowers on the ends of wiry spikes, sometimes more than once a year.

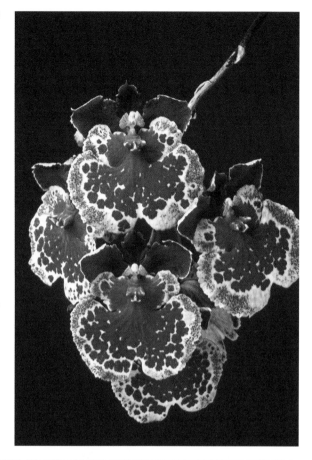

TOP From plants like *Tolumnia* Memoria Ralph Yagi, breeders have worked to create intense spotted and patterned flowers.

RIGHT The enormous color range of *Tolumnia* hybrids includes various sunset shades, as seen in *Tolumnia* Dorothy Oka 'Rocky'.

ABOVE Hybridizers have increased the size of miniature *Tolumnia* flowers from 1/2-inch blooms. The fan-shaped ruffled lips of *Tolumnia* Talisman 'Big Joe' are over 1 inch in diameter.

LEFT *Tolumnia* Popoki 'Mitzi' is a vigorous and floriferous selection popular for its vibrant magenta blooms.

Vanda

With their brightly colored and patterned flowers, *Vanda* orchids and their related hybrids have always been popular in warmer areas of the world, where the plants are often cultivated outside. Along with the rainbow of colors available in this group, some of the hybrids offer the elusive shades of blue and violet. Many *Vanda* hybrids can get quite large over time and require lots of space, but breeders have worked to produce compact floriferous plants as well.

TEMPERATURE
Day 70–85°F
Night 60–70°F

Native to humid forests of India, Thailand, Indonesia, the Philippines, and many other Pacific Islands, the genus *Vanda* consists of miniature to large epiphytes. The humid forests they come from have warm temperatures year-round, and in tropical areas of the world they are grown outdoors. Some of the modern hybrids incorporating *Vanda coerulea* have helped make the plants more tolerant of temperatures close to 50°F, but they grow and flower best with even warm temperatures year-round.

LIGHT
Although *Vanda* species and their related hybrids prefer bright light, they still require some shade to protect the plants from the strongest direct sunlight. The plants do best in a sunny window or greenhouse location and in warmer climates grow well outdoors. In more temperate climates, the plants can be summered outdoors in part shade, where they will appreciate the warmer humid conditions. This group has been hybridized extensively with related genera. Depending on the pedigree of the hybrid, some enjoy more sun and others can tolerate shadier conditions. Plants with narrow terete foliage tolerate warmer conditions, and those with *Neofinetia, Rhynchostylis*, or *Ascocentrum* in their background grow and bloom well in lower light conditions.

WATER
Vanda orchids enjoy abundant watering at their roots. Regular watering almost daily in warmer months is preferred, but with good drainage and air circulation to allow the roots to dry by night.

HUMIDITY

Vanda orchids prefer to grow in humidity conditions above 65% year-round. With their preference to have their roots exposed and open to the air, give the plants constant humidity for the best growth and flowering. Low humidity slows root growth and sometimes impedes the flowers from opening properly.

POTTING AND POTTING MIX

Vanda orchids and their relatives need an open coarse mix for the large and sometimes extensive roots to grow properly. These plants are often grown in slatted orchid baskets with little or no medium to allow the roots to be freely exposed to the air. Plants can be grown potted in smaller containers with excellent drainage and a large chunky mix, such as lava or volcanic rock or pieces of charcoal or bark. Many people grow the plants with no medium at all, instead hanging them from wire hooks or plastic baskets with the roots completely exposed and hanging free. These methods for potting allow for the proper balance of air around the roots and regular heavy watering that the plants require.

FERTILIZER

Vanda orchids are relatively heavy feeders. They benefit from regular feeding with a balance fertilizer at one-quarter to one-half strength almost weekly during warmer months, when the plants are actively growing. Fertilizer can be reduced slightly in the winter months. Supplemental feedings with seaweed and fish emulsion during the summer months can help to build healthy root systems and flowers.

PESTS AND DISEASES

Vanda orchids are relatively pest free. Mealybugs or scale might occasionally show up on the plants, but the main pests are thrips, which can attach the tender new foliage, roots, and flowers, especially in the warm months.

CULTURE NOTES AND TIPS

- Pot *Vanda* orchids in small containers or allow their roots to be exposed to the atmosphere.
- Provide the plants with regular watering, high humidity, and regular feeding during their growing season.
- In temperate climates, summer the plants outdoors in partial shade.

Vanda Cherry Blossom

syn. *Ascofinetia* Cherry Blossom

V.

Few miniature vandaceous hybrids can compete with the ease of culture and profuse blooming habit of this hybrid. *Vanda* Cherry Blossom is still a popular plant in orchid collections, almost 50 years after its original introduction. The combination of two miniature species, the brightly colored *Vanda ampullacea* (syn. *Ascocentrum ampullacea*) and the compact and fragrant *Vanda falcata* (syn. *Neofinetia falcata*), resulted in a delightful and aptly named hybrid. The quick-growing and clumping fans of foliage are adorned with profuse clusters of light pink blooms that resemble the namesake cherry blossoms. It grows well alongside other vandaceous orchids and even does well in slightly lower light conditions. It is a perfect plant for a windowsill or under lights.

Vanda falcata

syn. *Neofinetia falcata*

V.

Prized in Japan for hundreds of years, *Vanda falcata* is one of the most celebrated of Japanese native orchids. The diminutive plants are often cultivated solely for the beauty and arrangement of their leaves, and serious collectors will pay enormous sums for special forms. Fūkiran societies are devoted to the cultivation of this species and the multitudes of forms passed down through generations of cultivation in Japan. This species has also been used as a parent of many hybrids because of its floriferous, compact, and vigorous growth habit.

Despite their small size, the fragrant blooms of *Vanda falcata* can perfume an entire room.

Vanda falcata is a beautiful miniature plant that produces powerfully fragrant blooms, with the intoxicating fragrance described as a combination of coconut and jasmine. Even a small plant in bloom can perfume an entire room. It is an adaptable species that tolerates a wide range of temperatures and conditions, performing well either potted or mounted.

Vanda garayi

syn. *Ascocentrum garayi*

V.

This miniature species from Thailand has always been popular with orchidists for the compact fans of foliage that are crowned with dense spikes of electric orange flowers. *Vanda garayi* is a good choice for breeding miniature and compact *Vanda* hybrids, and many excellent hybrids have been produced. An easy plant to grow in limited space, it will thrive in a basket or container with an open mix to allow air around the root system. Over time, the plants form clumps of rigid fans of foliage, making this species attractive even out of bloom. Small specimens are hard to ignore, with their numerous spikes of flowers open all at once. The plants thrive in low light conditions and are excellent subjects for a windowsill.

This miniature *Vanda* species grows in clumps and produces upright spikes of bright orange flowers in early spring to summer.

Vanda Princess Mikasa

syn. *Ascocenda* Princess Mikasa

V.

Breeders have been able to replicate the intense blue violet-checkered flowers of *Vanda* orchids on more compact plants that can fit on a windowsill or in a smaller growing space. *Vanda* Princess Mikasa is offered in both the blue violet and magenta pink color forms, both brightly colored and with the classic checkered vanda patterns. The plants are compact and require similar conditions as other vandaceous hybrids. This selection does well in containers in a coarse mix with large bark and well-drained conditions.

Few other orchids produce blooms with the intense colors found in *Vanda* Princess Mikasa.

Vanda Princess Mikasa

Vanda Robert's Delight
V.

Of all the large-flowered *Vanda* hybrids, one of the best to come along in recent years is *Vanda* Robert's Delight. Several color forms have been released in the market, ranging from deep magenta pink to dark cranberry red, intense blue violet, and a dark purple/almost black flower. These large monopodial plants easily reach several feet tall and 24 inches from leaf tip to leaf tip and produce long cascading masses of roots. The plants are worth every effort and amount of space, as the large rounded blooms can be nearly 5 inches in diameter and with up to seven or eight blooms on each stem, creating an unforgettable sight. The plants require warm conditions and ample water and humidity throughout the year, but they are spectacular plants for a warm climate or greenhouse space.

With large colorful blooms, *Vanda* Robert's Delight is best grown in warm humid conditions and can be a challenge in the home.

Vandachostylis Lou Sneary
syn. *Neostylis* Lou Sneary
Van.

This is an excellent beginner plant for someone looking for those elusive blues that *Vanda* orchids possess without the requirement for a lot of space. *Vandachostylis* Lou Sneary is a compact plant with the color and fragrance of larger *Vanda* hybrids. The beautiful fans of foliage are themselves attractive, and the plant bears short sprays of crystalline blue violet flowers that resemble the *Vanda falcata* parent in shape. It is a free-flowering plant that blooms more than once per year when conditions are right. *Vandachostylis* Lou Sneary is easy to grow and does well in warm, lower light conditions alongside phalaenopsis and paphiopedilums.

The compact plants of *Vandachostylis* Lou Sneary make delightful fragrant specimens over time.

Zygolum Louisendorf 'Rhein Moonlight'
Zyglm.

This plant is an unusual and floriferous intergeneric hybrid between a *Zygopetalum* and a relatively obscure relative. *Zygolum* Louisendorf 'Rhein Moonlight' is a reliable grower and bloomer, often producing flowers more than once a year when healthy. The spidery green flowers have a large velvety maroon lip and have inherited some of the strong floral fragrance from *Zygopetalum*. This vigorous hybrid is grows and flowers well in warm conditions with even moisture and fertilizer throughout the year. The thin-leaved plants enjoy bright light and produce thick roots that grow best in a coarse bark mix or loose sphagnum moss.

Zygopetalum Hybrids
Zygo.

Bred from a group of warm-growing South American species, *Zygopetalum* hybrids are prized by aficionados for several reasons. The dark chestnut spotted sepals and petals provide an excellent foil for the intense blue violet velvet-textured lip, a rare color in the orchid family. During the day, they smell intensely of hyacinth and are among the most fragrant of orchids despite their smaller stature. *Zygopetalum* orchids are warm growers with glossy bright green foliage, doing well in *Phalaenopsis*-type conditions. The thin foliage can be prone to fungal spotting, so ensure the foliage is dry before nightfall.

Zygopetalum hybrids are celebrated for the blue-violet velvet patterns of the flower along with strong floral fragrances.

RESOURCES

VENDORS

Andy's Orchids
734 Ocean View Avenue
Encinitas, CA 92024
andysorchids.com
Wide variety of species orchids
including miniatures both potted and
mounted

Cal-Orchids
1251 Orchid Drive
Santa Barbara, CA 93111
calorchid.com
Miscellaneous hybrids, *Cattleya*,
Neofinetia, Epidendrum, Angraecum,
and other African species

Carter & Holmes Orchids
629 State Road S-36-273
Newberry, SC 29108
carterandholmes.com
Cattleya and other
miscellaneous orchids

Exotic Orchids of Maui
3141 Ua Noe Place
Haiku, HI 96708
mauiorchids.com
Species, *Cattleya*, and other
miscellaneous orchids

Far Reaches Farm
1818 Hastings Avenue
Port Townsend, WA 98368
farreachesfarm.com
Hardy garden orchids

Gardens at Post Hill
433 W Morris Road
Morris, CT 06763
gardensatposthill.net
Hardy garden orchids

Gold Country Orchids
390 Big Ben Road
Lincoln, CA 95648
goldcountryorchids.com
Cattleya, miniatures, and
miscellaneous species

Hillsview Gardens
13720 S. Mulino Road
Mulino, OR 97042
hillsviewgardens.com
Paphiopedilum

H&R Nurseries
41-240 Hihimanu Street
Waimanalo, HI 96795
hrnurseries.com
Miscellaneous species and hybrids,
Cattleya, Dendrobium

J&L Orchids
20 Sherwood Road
Easton, CT 06612
jlorchids.com
Miniatures, miscellaneous
species and hybrids

Kawamoto Orchid Nursery
2630 Waiomao Road
Honolulu, HI 96816
kawamotoorchids.com
Miscellaneous species and hybrids

Kelly's Korner Orchid Supplies
PO Box 539
Milford, NH 03055
kkorchid.com
Orchid-growing and potting supplies

Mountain Orchids
8 Pierce Road
North Springfield, VT 05150
mountainorchids.com
Miniature and cool-growing orchids

Norman's Orchid Nursery
11039 Monte Vista Avenue
Montclair, CA 91763
orchids.com

Phalaenopsis, Cattleya, Dendrobium, Oncidium, miscellaneous species and hybrids

Odom's Orchids
1611 S Jenkins Road
Fort Pierce, FL 34947
odoms.com

Cattleya and miscellaneous orchids

OFE International
17899 SW 280th Street
Homestead, FL 33031
ofeintl.com

Orchid-growing and potting supplies

Orchids by Hausermann's
2N134 Addison Road
Villa Park, IL 60181
orchidsbyhausermann.com

Cattleya, species, and miscellaneous hybrids

Orchids Limited
4630 Fernbrook Lane N
Plymouth, MN 55446
orchidweb.com

Paphiopedilum, Phragmipedium, Neofinetia, miscellaneous species and hybrids

Piping Rock Orchids
2270 Cook Road
Galway, NY 12074
pipingrockorchids.com

Paphiopedilum, Phragmipedium, miscellaneous species and hybrids

Plant Delights Nursery
9241 Sauls Road
Raleigh, NC 27603
plantdelights.com

Cypripedium and hardy garden orchids

Repotme.com
21657 Paradise Road
Georgetown, DE 19947
repotme.com

Orchid-growing and potting supplies

R.F. Orchids
28100 SW 182 Avenue
Homestead, FL 33030
rforchids.com

Vanda, Cattleya, miscellaneous species and hybrids

Santa Barbara Orchid Estate
1250 Orchid Drive
Santa Barbara, CA 93111
sborchid.com

Cymbidium, Cattleya, Laelia, miscellaneous species and hybrids

Seed Engei
seed-engei.com

Japanese orchids, *Neofinetia*

Sunset Valley Orchids
1255 Navel Place
Vista, CA 92081
sunsetvalleyorchids.com

Cattleya, Paphiopedilum, Catasetum hybrids

Tropical Orchid Farm
Hana Highway
Haiku, HI 96708
tropicalorchidfarm.com

Species orchids

Waldor Orchids
10 E Poplar Avenue
Linwood, NJ 08221
waldor.com

Cattleya, Dendrobium, Oncidium, miscellaneous species and hybrids

PUBLIC GARDENS WITH ORCHID DISPLAYS

Montreal Botanical Garden
4101 Rue Sherbrooke E
Montréal, QC H1X 2B2, Canada
m.espacepourlavie.ca/en/
botanical-garden

Brooklyn Botanic Garden
990 Washington Avenue
Brooklyn, NY 11225
bbg.org

The New York Botanical Garden
2900 Southern Boulevard
Bronx, NY 10458
nybg.org

**Phipps Conservatory and
Botanical Gardens**
1 Schenley Drive
Pittsburgh, PA 15213
phipps.conservatory.org

Longwood Gardens
1001 Longwood Road
Kennett Square, PA 19348
longwoodgardens.org

U.S. Botanic Garden
100 Maryland Avenue SW
Washington, DC 20001
usbg.gov

Atlanta Botanical Garden
1345 Piedmont Avenue NE
Atlanta, GA 30309
atlantabg.org

Fairchild Tropical Garden
10901 Old Cutler Road
Coral Gables, FL 33156
fairchildgarden.org

Marie Selby Botanical Garden
900 S Palm Avenue
Sarasota, FL 34236
Selby.org

Missouri Botanical Garden
4344 Shaw Boulevard
St. Louis, MO 63110
missouribotanicalgarden.org

Chicago Botanic Garden
1000 Lake Cook Road
Glencoe, IL 60022
chicagobotanic.org

Denver Botanic Gardens
1007 York Street
Denver, CO 80206
botanicgardens.org

**Huntington Library, Art
Collection, and Botanical Garden**
1151 Oxford Road
San Marino, CA 91108
huntington.org

**Conservatory of Flowers,
Golden Gate Park**
100 John F. Kennedy Drive
San Francisco, CA 94118
conservatoryofflowers.org

Royal Botanical Gardens, Kew
Kew, London Borough of
Richmond upon Thames
Richmond TW9 3AB, UK
kew.org

Royal Botanic Garden Edinburgh
Arboretum Place
Edinburgh EH3 5NZ, UK
rbge.org.uk

Eric Young Orchid Foundation
Moulin de Ponterrin Street,
Victoria Village
Trinity JE3 5HH, Jersey, UK
ericyoungorchid.org

**Kirstenbosch National
Botanical Garden**
Rhodes Drive, Newlands
Cape Town, 7735, South Africa
sanbi.org/gardens/kirstenbosch

Gardens by the Bay Singapore
18 Marina Gardens Drive
Singapore 018953
gardensbythebay.com.sg

Singapore Botanic Gardens
1 Cluny Road
Singapore 259569
nparks.gov.sg/sbg

Nong Nooch Tropical Botanical Garden
34/1 Tambon Na Chom Thian,
Amphoe Sattahip
Chang Wat Chon Buri 20250,
Thailand
nongnoochtropicalgarden.com

Queen Sirkit Botanical Garden
9 Mae Raem, Amphoe Mae Rim
Chang Wat Chiang Mai 50180,
Thailand
qsbg.org

Ran No Yakata, Nagoya's Orchid Garden
4 Chome-4-1 Osu
Naka Ward, Nagoya, Aichi 460-0011,
Japan
flarie.jp

ORGANIZATIONS AND ONLINE FORUMS

American Orchid Society
aos.org
Fairchild Tropical Botanic Garden
10901 Old Cutler Road
Coral Gables FL 33156

One of the best resources for information on home orchid growing, local orchid societies, orchid judging, and orchid information in the United States and around the world

Orchid Board
orchidboard.com
Online orchid discussion forum where enthusiasts gather and share information and images

Orchids Forum
orchidsforum.com
Discussion forums for amateur and professional orchid growers

Orchid Mall
orchidmall.com
Collection of links to nurseries, orchid resources, orchid societies, and classified ads

OrchidWire
orchidwire.com
Collection of Web links about orchids, orchid societies, and nurseries

PHOTO & ILLUSTRATION CREDITS

Greg Allikas — orchidworks.com, pages 18, 20, 25 top, 28 left,
34, 49, 152, 153 bottom, 154 top, 155, 161, 163, 164, 169, 172, 173,
178, 179 bottom, 180, 181, 184 top, 185, 188, 189, 192, 193, 196, 197 bottom,
200, 203, 204, 205, 209, 212, 213, 214, 217, 219, 220, 221, 222 bottom,
223 top, 224, 225, 228, 229, 232, 233, 234, 235

Marc Hachadourian, pages 35, 78

Eric Hunt, pages 22, 77, 153 top, 154 bottom, 165, 184 bottom, 201, 202

iStock.com/lanolin, page 26

Charles Marden Fitch, pages 28 right, 179 top, 197 right

Duane McDowell, page 21

The New York Botanical Garden, pages 13, 17, 197 top left, 222 top

Robert Pavlis, author of GardenMyths.com, page 62 top

Photo collages on pages 80–89 and all other images by Claire Rosen.

Illustrations on page 19 by Alan Bryan.

INDEX

A

abbreviations, 29
Acianthera pubescens, 219
Aerangis luteoalba var. *rhodosticta*, 152
Africa, 152
agar, 16
air circulation, 40–42, 49
Aliceara, 27, 28
   Marfitch, 27
   Marfitch 'Howards Dream', 196
   Tahoma Glacier, 196
American Orchid Society (AOS), 28
anatomy, 20–24
Angraecum sesquipedale, 152
Anoectochilus, 17, 25
Anoectochilus formosanus, 184
antelope dendrobiums, 177
aphids, 75, 160, 167, 171, 187, 195, 211, 216, 227
aphrodisiac, 12, 17
Aristotle, 12
aroids, 22
artificial lights, 35–36
"art shades", 223
Asarum, 10
Ascocenda Princess Mikasa, 233
Ascocentrum ampullacea, 232
Ascocentrum garayi, 233
Ascofinetia, Cherry Blossom, 232
Award of Merit (AM), 28
awards, 28
Aztecs, 12, 17

B

bacterial diseases, 75, 88
baskets, 48–49

Bhutan, 206
Bletilla, 77
Bletilla striata, 77
Bolivia, 161
bonsai tree, 114–119
boron (B), 44
Brassanthe Maikai 'Mayumi', 153
Brassavola, 27
   Little Stars, 153
Brassavola cordata, 154
Brassavola nodosa, 27, 153, 154
Brassia, 27, 194, 196
   Rex, 154
Brassolaeliocattleya
   Burdekin Wonder, 223
   George King 'Serendipity', 223
   Goldenzelle 'Lemon Chiffon', 224
   Malworth 'Orchidglade', 224
Brassolaeliocattleya Melody Fair 'Carol', 163
Brazil, 18, 161, 163, 185, 215
bromeliads, 22
Bulbophyllum Elizabeth Ann 'Buckle-berry', 152
butterfly orchid, 13

C

cacti, 22
Calanthe, 78
California, 79
Cameroon, 152
Catasetum, 156–157, 180
Cattleya, 22, 27, 33, 36, 39, 47, 50, 53, 62, 68, 77, 79, 158–160, 179, 221, 222, 224
   Canhamiana 'Azure Skies', 160
   Dinard 'Blue Heaven', 161

Drumbeat 'Heritage', 162
   Mari's Song, 162
   Melody Fair 'Carol', 163
   Mini Purple, 27, 163
Cattleya cernua, 160
Cattleya maxima, 28
Cattleya mossiae, 160
Cattleya trianae, 12
Cattleytonia Why Not, 181
Cattlianthe
   Gold Digger 'Fuchs Mandarin', 164
   Jewel Box 'Scheherazade', 164
Central America, 11, 156, 180, 181, 189, 194, 215, 220, 222, 225
ceramic pots, 48
charcoal, 50
chemical fertilizers, 44
Chile, 51
China, 10, 21, 169, 200, 203, 206
"chocolate orchid", 196
clonal name, 28
Clowesia, 156, 180
   Rebecca Northen 'Pink Grapefruit', 165
coconut fiber/chunks, 51–52
collection, 33
Colombia, 11, 12, 179, 185
commercial production, 16
conservation, 25
containers, 46–49
Costa Rica, 11, 12, 18
cultivar, 28
cultivation, 10–15
cutting, 47
Cycnoches, 156
Cymbidium, 16, 22, 39, 47, 53, 79, 85, 166–167
   Compact Hybrids, 168

Dorothy Stockstill 'Forgotten Fruit', 168

Golden Elf, 169

Sara Jean 'Ice Cascade', 28, 169

Cymbidium devonianum, 168

Cypripedium, 77

D

Dactylorhiza, 78

dancing lady orchids, 194–197

Darwin, Charles, 13–15, 152

decorative orchid terrarium, 96–101

Dendrobium, 10, 22, 39, 50, 53, 54, 62, 79, 170–171

Burana Green 'First Chance', 172

Burana Jade, 172

Burana Sapphire, 172

Burana Stripe, 172

Emma White, 172

Enobi Purple 'Splash', 173

Frosty Dawn, 173

Hard Cane Type Hybrids, 172

Micro Chip, 174

Quique Ramirez 'Karen's Delight', 172

Roy Tokunaga, 177

Samurai, 177

Dendrobium aberrans, 174

Dendrobium aemulum, 22

Dendrobium heterocarpum, 175

Dendrobium kingianum, 174

Dendrobium nobile, 17, 175–176

Dendrobium regium, 175

Dendrobium spectabile, 178

Dendrochilum magnum, 178

diseases

Catasetum, 157

Cattleya, 160

common, 72, 75

Cymbidium, 167

Dendrobium, 171

Dendrobium nobile, 176

fall care, 88

jewel orchids, 183

Masdevallia, 187

Miltoniopsis, 191

Oncidium, 195

Paphiopedilum, 199

Phaius, 208

Phalaenopsis, 211

Phragmipedium, 216

Tolumnia, 227

Vanda, 231

dividing, 55–67

dondurma, 17

Douglas fir, 50

drainage, 32, 37, 39, 46, 48, 49, 50, 51, 55

Dresslerella pilosissima, 18

E

Ecuador, 18

Encyclia cochleata, 220

Encyclia cordigera, 179

England, 12–15

Epidendrum, 29

Epidendrum peperomia, 179

epiphytes, 21–22, 29, 37

epiphytic orchid potting recipe mix, 53

Equitant *Oncidium*, 226

ethnobotanical use, 11–12

Euchile citrina, 11

Europe, 12

F

fall care, 88

feeding, 43–46

ferns, 22, 99

fertilizers

Catasetum, 157

Cattleya, 159–160

Cymbidium, 167

Dendrobium, 171

Dendrobium nobile, 176

fall care, 88

jewel orchids, 183

Miltoniopsis, 191

Oncidium, 195

Paphiopedilum, 199

Phaius, 208

Phalaenopsis, 211

Phragmipedium, 216

Tolumnia, 227

types of, 44–45

Vanda, 231

fir bark, 50

Fittonia, 99

Florida, 79, 194, 220, 224

flowers

cutting, 47

diversity, 18–20

floral structure, 19–20

jewel orchids, 25

fluorescent lights, 35–36

foliage, 10–11, 21, 25, 34, 78, 211

fragrance, 20

Fredclarkeara After Dark, 180

Fūkiran, 21

fungal diseases, 75, 88

furan, 21

G

Gastrochilus retrocalla, 180

genus, 27

germination techniques, 16

Gomesa, 196

Goodyera pubescens, 25

Grammatophyllum speciosum, 18

growing environment

home, 30–53

outdoors, 76–79

growing on mount, 68–71

Guarianthe bowringiana, 153

Guarianthe skinneri, 11, 12

Guaritonia Why Not, 181

H

habitats, 17, 20–22
hanging gallery, 144–149
Haraella retrocalla, 180
Hepatica, 10
high-intensity discharge (HID) lights, 36
Highly Commendable Certificate (HCC), 28
Himalayas, 200
humidity
  Catasetum, 157
  Cattleya, 159
  Cymbidium, 167
  Dendrobium, 171
  Dendrobium nobile, 175–176
  fall care, 88
  jewel orchids, 183
  Masdevallia, 186–187
  Miltoniopsis, 191
  Oncidium, 195
  Paphiopedilum, 199
  Phaius, 207
  Phalaenopsis, 210
  Phragmipedium, 216
  spring care, 85
  Tolumnia, 226
  Vanda, 231
  watering and, 37–42
  winter care, 82
hyacinth orchid, 77
hybrids, 15, 27–28, 33, 152, 172, 173, 177, 188, 192–193, 202, 204, 206, 209, 213, 218, 228–229, 233, 235

I

India, 200, 201, 206
Indonesia, 18
inorganic fertilizers, 44, 45
iron (Fe), 44

J

Jamaica, 181
Japan, 10–11, 21, 232
Japan Orchid Growers Association (JOGA), 28
jewel orchids, 25, 182–183, 184
jewel orchid terrarium, 92–95
jin xianlan, 17
Jones & Scully Orchidglade, 224

K

keiki, 54
Kenya, 152
Knudson, Lewis, 16
kokedama, 108–113
koten engei, 10

L

lady's slippers, 77, 201
Laelia, 27
Laelia anceps, 79
Laelia superbiens, 11
Laeliocattleya
  Dinard 'Blue Heaven', 161
  Drumbeat 'Heritage', 162
  Gold Digger 'Fuchs Mandarin', 164
  Mari's Song, 162
Latin America, 11–12
Leomesezia Lava Burst 'Puanani', 184
Leptotes bicolor, 49, 185
light
  Catasetum, 156
  Cattleya, 158–159
  Cymbidium, 166
  Dendrobium, 170
  Dendrobium nobile, 175
  fall care, 88
  growing conditions and, 32–36
  jewel orchids, 182

  Masdevallia, 186
  Miltoniopsis, 190
  Oncidium, 194
  Paphiopedilum, 198
  Phaius, 207
  Phalaenopsis, 210
  Phragmipedium, 215
  Tolumnia, 226
  Vanda, 230
light-emitting diode (LED) lights, 36
Lockhartia oerstedii, 185
Ludisia, 25
Ludisia discolor, 25, 184

M

Macodes, 25
Macodes petola, 184
macronutrients, 43–44
Madagascar, 152
manganese (Mn), 44
Masdevallia, 87, 88, 97, 186–187, 218
  Cinnamon Gold, 188
  Copper Angel, 188
  hybrids, 188
  Ken Dole, 188
  Mary Staal, 188
  Pat Akehurst 'Golden Zebra', 189
  Peach Fuzz, 188
  Sinichi Komoda, 188
Masdevallia floribunda, 188
Masdevallia infracta, 188
Masdevallia tonduzii, 188
Masdevallia veitchiana, 189
Maxillaria tenuifolia, 189
mealybugs, 75, 160, 171, 183, 187, 191, 199, 208, 211, 216, 227, 231
medicinal orchids, 10, 11, 17
Mediterranean region, 12
Mexico, 11, 185, 189, 222
micronutrients, 44
Miltassia, 27

Miltonia, 27, 194, 196
Miltoniopsis, 50, 85, 87, 88, 190–191
  Bert Field, 192
  hybrids, 192–193
  Martin Orenstein, 193
  Sierra Snows 'Colomborquideas', 193
Miltoniopsis vexillaria, 11
miniature mobile, 132–138
miniature orchids, 33, 50, 132–138, 152, 169, 179, 232
monopodial orchids, 22, 23, 56–61
Monterey pine tree, 50
Morel, Georges, 16
Mormodes, 156, 180

N

name changes, 29
names, 27–29
national flowers, 12
Neofinetia falcata, 11, 232
Neostylis Lou Sneary, 234
New Guinea, 177, 178
New Zealand, 51
nitrogen (N), 43, 45
nobile dendrobiums, 175–176
nurseries, 25

O

Odontobrassia, 27
Oncidium, 22, 27, 39, 47, 50, 53, 62, 87, 194–197
  Alliance, 196
  Gower Ramsey, 196
  intergenerics, 194–197
  Sharry Baby, 196
  Sharry Baby 'Sweet Fragrance', 196
  Tiger Crow 'Golden Girl', 197
Oncostele Wildcat, 196, 197
orchid fever, 13
orchid ice cream, 17
orchid wreath, 102–107

organic fertilizers, 44–45
orkhis, 12
osmunda fiber, 49
outdoor gardens, 76–79
overwatering, 76

P

Pacific Northwest, 79
palms, 10
Panama, 12, 185
pansy orchid, 192
Paphiopedilum, 29, 36, 39, 50, 85, 97, 127, 174, 185, 188, 198–199
  Bob Nagel 'New Horizon', 204
  British Concorde 'Crystelle', 200
  complex hybrids, 200
  Greyi, 202
  Hellas, 200
  hybrids, 204, 206
  Julius, 202
  Julius 'Kiaora', 34
  Lynleigh Koopowitz, 203
  Maudiae hybrids, 204
  Maudiae 'Magnificum', 28
  Olympic Spots, 200
  Pinocchio, 204
  Raingreen's Legend, 204
  Saint Swithin, 205
  Valerie Tonkin, 200
  Winston Churchill, 200
Paphiopedilum delenatii, 201, 203
Paphiopedilum exul, 200
Paphiopedilum godefroyae, 202
Paphiopedilum gratrixianum, 201
Paphiopedilum insigne, 200, 201
Paphiopedilum lowii, 202
Paphiopedilum niveum, 202
Paphiopedilum philippinense, 205
Paphiopedilum rothschildianum, 202, 205
Paphiopedilum spicerianum, 206
Paphiopedilum vietnamense, 25

Paphiopedilum villosum, 200, 201
"paphs", 29
Paraguay, 161
penjing, 120–125
Peperomia, 99
Peristeria elata, 12
perlite, 51
Peru, 28
pests
  Catasetum, 157
  Cattleya, 160
  common, 72, 75
  Cymbidium, 167
  Dendrobium, 171
  Dendrobium nobile, 176
  fall care, 88
  jewel orchids, 183
  Masdevallia, 187
  Miltoniopsis, 191
  Oncidium, 195
  Paphiopedilum, 199
  Phaius, 208
  Phalaenopsis, 211
  Phragmipedium, 216
  Tolumnia, 227
  Vanda, 231
Phaius, 207–208
  hybrids, 209
  Microburst 'Orchtoberfest', 209
Phaius tankervillae, 209
Phalaenopsis, 16, 22, 29, 34, 36, 47, 50, 54, 56, 79, 85, 103, 152, 174, 185, 194, 210–211, 235
  Baldan's Kaleidoscope 'Golden Treasure', 212
  Brother Orange Runabout, 213
  Doris, 214
  hybrids, 213
  Sogo Yukidian, 214
  Surf Song, 213
  Taisuco Swan, 213

Index

Phalaenopsis bellina, 212
Phalaenopsis schilleriana, 214
"phals", 29
Philippines, 178
Philodendron, 99
phosphorus (P), 44, 45
Phragmipedium, 39, 47, 53, 215–216
   Don Wimber, 217
   Grande, 217
   hybrids, 218
   Memoria Dick Clements, 218
   Sedenii, 218
Phragmipedium besseae, 218
Phragmipedium sargentianum, 218
Pilea, 99
placement, 32–34
plant diversity, 15, 18–20
plant growth, 34
plant nutrition, 43–44
plant problems, 72–74
plastic pots, 46
Platystele jungermannioides, 18
pleurothallids, 218
Pleurothallis grobyi, 218–219
Pleurothallis nossax, 219
Pleurothallis ornata, 218
Pleurothallis pubescens, 219
Pleurothallis tribuloides, 218
Pleurothallis truncata, 219
pollinators, 19–20
potassium (K), 44, 45
pots, 46–48
potting mixes
   Catasetum, 157
   Cattleya, 159
   Cymbidium, 167
   Dendrobium, 171
   Dendrobium nobile, 176
   jewel orchids, 183
   Masdevallia, 187
   Miltoniopsis, 191

Oncidium, 195
Paphiopedilum, 199
Phaius, 207–208
Phalaenopsis, 211
Phragmipedium, 216
Tolumnia, 227
types of, 49–53
Vanda, 231
projects
   bonsai tree, 114–119
   decorative orchid terrarium, 96–101
   hanging gallery, 144–149
   jewel orchid terrarium, 92–95
   kokedama, 108–113
   miniature mobile, 132–138
   orchid wreath, 102–107
   penjing, 120–125
   sculpture, 138–143
   woodland garden orchid centerpiece, 127–131
propagating, 54
Prosthechea cochleate, 220
pseudobulbs, 22, 24
Psychopsis, 13
   Kahili, 220
Psychopsis papilio, 14

Q

queen of the night orchid, 154

R

Renanthera Kalsom 'Red Dragon', 221
repotting, 55–67, 160
Rhapis, 10
Rhyncattleanthe
   Burana Beauty, 221
   Dan O'Neil 'Jubilee', 222
Rhyncholaelia digbyana, 27, 222
Rhyncholaeliocattleya
   Burdekin Wonder, 223
   George King 'Serendipity', 223

   Goldenzelle 'Lemon Chiffon', 224
   Malworth 'Orchidglade', 224
Rhynchostylis gigantea, 20, 225
root disease, 72–76
roots, 22–24, 51

S

salep, 17
Sarcoglottis, 25
scale insects, 75, 160, 167, 171, 199, 208, 211, 216, 227, 231
sculpture, 138–143
seedling bark, 50
seeds, 16, 18–19
semi-terrestrial orchids, 215
shi hu, 17
sick plant rehabilitation, 72
slow-release fertilizers, 45, 159–160, 171
slugs, 75, 88, 183
snails, 75, 88, 160, 183
Sophrolaeliocattleya Jewel Box 'Scheherazade', 164
Sophronitis cernua, 161
South America, 11, 156, 179, 180, 194, 215, 220, 235
Southeast Asia, 175
species, 18, 27, 33
Specklinia, 218
Specklinia grobyi, 218–219
Specklinia tribuloides, 218–219
sphagnum moss, 51, 54, 76
spider mites, 75, 157, 167, 183, 187, 191, 195, 199, 208, 211, 227
spider orchids, 154
Spiranthes, 78
Spiranthes odorata 'Chadds Ford', 78
Spiranthes speciosa, 25, 225
Splash Petal cattleyas, 162
sponge rock, 51
spring care, 85
Stanhopea tigrina, 11

Stelis, 218

Stelis ornata, 218–219

Stewart Orchids, 162

summer care, 87

sympodial orchids, 16, 22, 62–67

T

Taiwan, 180

temperate climates, 76–78

temperature
    Catasetum, 156
    Cattleya, 158
    Cymbidium, 166, 167
    Dendrobium, 170
    Dendrobium nobile, 175
    fall care, 88
    groups, 42–43
    jewel orchids, 182
    Masdevallia, 186
    Miltoniopsis, 190
    Oncidium, 194
    Paphiopedilum, 198
    Phaius, 207
    Phalaenopsis, 210
    Phragmipedium, 215
    spring care, 85
    Tolumnia, 226
    Vanda, 230
    winter care, 82

terra cotta pots, 39, 48

terrestrial orchid potting recipe mix, 53

terrestrial orchids, 12, 17, 21, 25, 50, 77, 166, 183, 198, 207–208, 209, 225

Thailand, 221

Theophrastus, 12

thrips, 75, 160, 208, 227, 231

Tolumnia, 68, 226–227
    Dorothy Oka 'Rocky', 228
    hybrids, 228–229
    Popoki 'Mitzi', 229
    Ralph Yagi, 228

tropical climates, 79

Turkey, 17

U

United States, 15, 16

V

Vanda, 16, 22, 23, 27, 36, 39, 47, 49, 50, 53, 56, 79, 87, 88, 152, 230–231
    Cherry Blossom, 232
    hybrids, 233, 234
    Lou Sneary, 234
    Princess Mikasa, 233
    Princess Mikasa × Robert's Delight, 28
    Robert's Delight, 234

Vanda ampullacea, 232

Vanda falcata, 11, 21, 232

Vanda garayi, 233

vanilla, 12, 17

Vanilla, 17, 18

Vanilla planifolia, 17

Venezuela, 28, 179

Vietnam, 25, 201, 203

viruses, 75

W

watering
    Catasetum, 156–157
    Cattleya, 159
    Cymbidium, 166
    Dendrobium, 170
    Dendrobium nobile, 175
    humidity and, 37–40
    jewel orchids, 182
    Masdevallia, 186
    Miltoniopsis, 190
    Oncidium, 194
    overwatering, 76
    Paphiopedilum, 198
    Phaius, 207
    Phalaenopsis, 210

Phragmipedium, 215

Tolumnia, 226

Vanda, 230

"weekly weakly" adage, 46

Wells, H. G., 9

wild ginger, 10

wild plants, 25

winter care, 82

woodland garden orchid centerpiece, 127–131

Z

Zygolum Louisendorf 'Rhein Moonlight', 235

Zygopetalum hybrids, 235

© Chris Kozarich

Marc Hachadourian is the director of glasshouse horticulture and senior curator of orchids at the New York Botanical Garden, overseeing the cultivation of tens of thousands of tropical and temperate plants grown for conservatory exhibitions and permanent horticultural display. He also serves as the curator of the garden's orchid collection. Marc oversees the CITES Rescue Center Program for the garden, helping to take in and rehabilitate plants that have been illegally imported, to conserve and protect endangered species.